Mario I. Aguilar occupies a chair in divinity at the University of St Andrews, Scotland. Born in Santiago, Chile, he experienced at a young age, and together with his extended family, the torture and killing of political opponents by the government of General Augusto Pinochet. He found his Christian vocation within the Catholic Church of that time, and he has worked with Christian communities in Chile and Kenya. He has lived in St Andrews since 1994, and over the years has led a contemplative life, while being involved with human-rights organizations and exiles. His academic research extends to Chile, Colombia, Kenya, Rwanda and Tibet, and he has recently completed, in three volumes, *The History and Politics of Latin American Theology* (SCM Press, 2007–8), and is working on the nine-volume *A Social History of the Catholic Church in Chile* (Edwin Mellen Press, four volumes published 2004–8; five volumes forthcoming).

CONTEMPLATING GOD, CHANGING THE WORLD

Mario I. Aguilar

SEABURY BOOKS
New York

Originally published in Great Britain in 2008 by
the Society for Promoting Christian Knowledge,
36 Causton Street, London SW1P 4ST.

© 2008 by Mario I. Aguilar
All rights reserved.

ISBN-13: 978–1–59627–108–1

A catalog record of this book is available from the Library of Congress.

First published in the United States of America in 2008 by
Seabury Books
445 Fifth Avenue
New York, New York 10016

www.seaburybooks.com

An imprint of Church Publishing Incorporated

Printed in the United Kingdom

5 4 3 2 1

This book is dedicated to my father,
whom I have missed for most of my life

Eheu fugaces labuntur anni

Contents

Acknowledgements

This book was written amid ongoing discussions about religion and politics within the academic community of the Centre for the Study of Religion and Politics (CSRP) of the University of St Andrews. I am grateful to Dr Ian Bradley and Dr Eric Stoddart, fellow theologians at St Mary's College, for encouraging this kind of writing, and to my doctoral students, who contributed with their own personal challenges to the sharpening of some of these ideas and Christian practices, particularly Jennifer Kilps, Jeff Tippner, Rob Whiteman, Jonathan Rowe, Yumi Murayama, Casey Nicholson, Gordon Barclay, Alissa Jones Nelson and her husband Matt, Joanne Wood, Alejandro Chávez and his wife Paloma, James Pitts and Ross Wissmann. I am thankful to Rebecca Mulhearn, commissioning editor at SPCK, for believing that a short conversation could become a book. My life as a contemplative has been supported by Laurel and Sara, and I hope that in reading this book they might understand me better.

Mario I. Aguilar
St Andrews

Introduction: issues in contemplation and politics today

———•◆•———

This book argues for a closer Christian relationship with contemplation as a form of prayer and of politics. Contemplation is, first, the act of being face to face with God in a moment of silence by becoming aware of his divine presence in order to stay still and draw from that presence; and second, it is the movement from the presence of God as a person to his presence in others, in the social and natural world. I shall focus on a few Christian figures of the twentieth century who were able to bridge their prayer life and their deep political commitment, and shall stress the role of the Eucharist as central to Christian contemplation, while extending the life of Christian prayer into society, arguing for a concrete involvement in politics from a Christian point of view. The theoretical purpose of this book is to encourage Christian engagement with social realities, and a greater sense of prayer and contemplation as tools to be used for that purpose by Christian communities and Christian activists in the UK and elsewhere.

Since the advent of the Second Vatican Council (1962–5) and the proclamation of the document *Gaudium et Spes* on the role of the Church in the modern world, there has been a refreshed and renewed involvement of Christians in the social and political world. That involvement has extended to participation in and formation of political parties, dialogue with other religions and dialogue with agnostics and atheists, and even a Christian presence among societies where Christianity is either a minority religion or only present through a few communities of missionaries, lay or religious.

Literature on Christian action and involvement with the poor and the marginalized, involvement with the secular world and with those who have fallen into the trap of consumerism, has dominated theological writing on the mission and action of the Church in the contemporary world. The same issues have influenced a Christian involvement in politics, where commitment to change in society has been expressed by the articulation of justice and peace groups, charity organizations and many different reflection groups, such as basic Christian communities[1] that have addressed the present and future of society.

Much less has been said about the possibility that all Christian action comes out of a deep communication with the divine that ultimately provides the motivation and the justification for such Christian action in society. I purposely use the expression 'said' because it is very clear that those communities that have been more involved in issues of justice and peace and in the politics of society, for example those in Latin America, have been deeply nourished by the celebration of the Eucharist and by communal prayer. Even if the general perception of social movements or movements for liberation relates to their action, it is clear that their Christian involvement in the world has arisen out of prayer and liturgical moments (communal celebrations of the Eucharist, pilgrimages and moments of common liturgical prayer of the Divine Office) in which they have conversed with God about the state of the world and about their own calling to get involved within that world, God's world. Without that communal and personal prayer, Gustavo Gutiérrez would not have written *A Theology of Liberation*, and Archbishop Oscar Romero would not have articulated a call to mutiny addressed to the army of El Salvador.[2]

Indeed, throughout the history of Christianity, those pastoral agents and religious communities who have been central to the renewal of Christianity in a locality or who heroically have spread Christianity over unknown lands have comprised men and women of prayer. Those who have embraced a deeper prayer and have spent some time in conversation and contemplation of God have been given not only courage and understanding to grow in personal holiness but also the courage to help others, to empathize with those suffering and to become one with God and with others. Those who have achieved a deeper level of contemplation have found consolation and energy to challenge the world and to propose radical changes within their contemporary societies. There is a connection between personal contemplation and political action that needs to be explored; there is a connection between personal contemplation and the changing of the world into a better, more just, more human and more divine world.

My own experience of having been born and raised in Chile was rather traumatic. My family had sympathizers with all political parties. While my grandfather was forced into early retirement when Salvador Allende took over the government in 1970, after the military coup of September 1973 my uncle was executed and several other relatives had to leave the country to stay alive. Secrecy was the order of the day, and I was involved with a left-wing political cell labelled by the military government as extremist. The experience of doing 'secret things' was exhilarating, but with a cruel result: all those I was involved with were arrested or fled, and my sweetheart, who was also involved with the cell, disappeared.

It was at that age – I was still a minor – that I discovered that the Catholic Church had some great practices: prayer, contemplation, solidarity and the defence of those persecuted by the military. I heard stories about priests, nuns and contemplative monks who sheltered the 'terrorists', and in my solitude I learned that God was always there. Much later, places of horror, such as the Villa Grimaldi, became parks of peace, and I returned several times to visit the grounds. Here, memories of the human, and bestial, screams of the prisoners also brought memories of God's voice, God's comfort and God's hope. It is clear to me that during those periods of extreme brutality, God was present, not as a witness, but as a prisoner, as a tortured and crucified body. The politics of social justice that brought many prisoners to centres of torture became the politics of God. Thus, contemplation and political activity became united; an experience that has moulded my contemplation of the past few years and that constitutes the paradigm behind the arguments of this book.

In this book I explore these connections by examining the following themes: first, within this introduction, some moments and movements of creative contemplation within the history of the Church that have marked our understanding of contemplation and politics; second, in the first six chapters, the lives and writings of a few Christian figures of the twentieth century who managed to integrate contemplation and politics by combining silence and activism. Third, I propose some ways in which to practise contemplation and politics in the contemporary world. I argue that in a post-9/11 era, the integration of Christian contemplation into political life, for those who are Christians, would make us into better images of God – true human beings who can experience God in everyday life, and better instruments of God by making us experience the realities of an internationally complex world that should be filled by the divine. Beside a human 'war on terror' there is another 'angel riding the storm',[3] and that is Christ, the centre of all Christian contemplation and politics.

The act of contemplation

The two BBC television series, *The Monastery* and *The Monastery Revisited*, first broadcast in 2005 and 2006 respectively, highlighted for the general public a relatively obscure Christian activity, namely contemplation.[4] Throughout the two series, Benedictine monks were able to explain their own communal life through the experience of welcoming 'public guests', here a group of men from different backgrounds who stayed with them and shared the long daily prayers, the silence and the solitude of a monastery where members of the religious community strive for union with Christ through prayer, study and work. Thus, that particular monastery became a media icon of many other communities of men and women who live together united by a common commitment to Christ in order to pursue the final and central goal of Christian human existence, which is to know Christ by spending time in prayer, meditation and contemplation.

Within that act of contemplation of divine realities, Christian practitioners seek a closer and deeper union with Christ and his person, while allowing for an ongoing Christian engagement with the world. The politics of contemplation can be summarized in two ways of being contemplative: within the world, and within the monastery. Those contemplatives within the world exercise their gifts of prayer and search for the divine within their daily activities and their work, while those attached to a monastery or to a community consecrate their own personal freedom to a community of contemplatives who live within enclosed walls and under a common rule that organizes their common prayer and their daily work.

While levels of contemplative engagement and of prayer vary according to individuals, the act of contemplation is a Christian activity exercised by all Christians, to the extent that they pray and read the Scriptures on their own or within a moment of communal worship. It arises out of the centrality of the Christ who calls all Christians to prayer, following his example of prayer to his Father.

Thomas Merton, commenting on the writings of St Bernard of Clairvaux, suggested that 'contemplation is simply the possession, by experience, of what we have read in Scripture'.[5] Thus, the human being who contemplates the person of the divine does not stand as a higher human being, as perceived by the Gnostics, but by having sustained deep moments of encounter with God seeks to follow the gospel more closely. As a result, contemplative lives are moved towards an apostolic life outside their ongoing contemplative experience. The experience of a sustained life of prayer, meditation and contemplation fills the everyday life; it is not a one-day observance of a liturgical obligation. The Scriptures are read and prayed upon every day (and hopefully several times a day), so that by acquiring a routine of prayer and detachment from the noises of the world, the contemplative comes naturally to appreciate what is central and becomes ever more detached from what is secondary to human life and to a fully lived Christian life.

Contemplation as a human act of communication and dialogue with the divine reflects a centuries-rich experience within the Church. Contemplatives emerged as rebels and challengers of a too worldly church community that throughout the Church's history, and particularly at certain times, became too close to human and political powers, thus forgetting the centrality of the Christ as Lord and of the Kingdom of God as a kingdom 'here' and 'not yet', somehow realized in the Church but still to be realized fully in Heaven.

Therefore, I argue that at particular moments within the history of the Church, those who sought solitude and a deeper encounter with God challenged the establishment and became symbols of divine realities, not only for the initiated and the learned, but for all. Mother Teresa and her Sisters of Charity became a clear example of a very active life helping those unwanted by society, but also of a contemplative community that spent long hours every day in communal and individual prayer and contemplative prayer. Each one of Mother Teresa's Sisters needed good health not only because of the intensity of their work with the poor and the marginalized but also because of the short hours of sleep and the long hours of prayer required by Mother Teresa and the leaders of each one of her communities.

Other contemporary contemplatives, for example James Conner OCSO, have reminded us that great contemplatives such as Thomas Merton defined contemplation 'as a simple awareness of the presence of God'.[6] If, for Conner, who is a Trappist monk at the Abbey of Gethsemani, Kentucky, 'the Eucharist is the preeminent place where we encounter the presence of God', it is possible to argue – and I do so in this book – that Christians of all traditions, sacramental and scriptural, can and need to exercise that 'simple awareness' in their daily lives. The history of the Church shows the beginnings and the development of monasticism as practical Christian challenge to moments of change, crisis and establishment, by which prophetic figures head for places of solitude and later form communities in order to remind the rest of the Church of the importance, centrality and primacy of God and the values of the Kingdom within the daily existence of a common humanity.

The Church and contemplation

Monasticism and the art of contemplation as a recognized charisma and way of life within the Church can be traced back to Anthony in Egypt, around the year 270 CE.[7] At that time Anthony, a twenty-year-old, entered a church building, gave away all his parents' inheritance and went to live in the desert in inaccessible tombs. He lived alone, prayed and supported his existence through manual labour. Others considered him very holy and some came to live near him to imitate his way of life.[8]

St Anthony's life was not easy: providing himself with enough food was difficult, he could not follow the rule of common prayer by then expected of all Christians, and as a hermit he developed psychological problems. At the same time, the monk Pachomius, who first developed the idea of 'the monastery',[9] started gathering his followers under a common rule by the Nile at Tabennisi, and the first monastic communities in Egypt started to flourish.[10] Later, different groups spread throughout Europe, with different understandings of the coenobitic life (life in common) due to the varied spiritual guidance offered by Augustine, Jerome and Ambrose.[11] Henry Chadwick has argued that 'there was an ideological tension between the hermit-ideal and the belief that the monastic life required a community under rule with obedience to a superior as an essential principle.'[12] Indeed, the start of monasticism raised questions about the aims of such life within the Church, about its project, discipline and challenge to the authority of the Church as a centralized body.[13]

The introduction of monasticism in the West can be traced back to the year 340 CE, when Athanasius visited Rome accompanied by the Egyptian monks Ammon and Isidore, both disciples of St Anthony. By 360 CE, St Martin had started monastic life at Ligugé near Poitiers, and after his consecration as Bishop of Tours built a monastery outside the city that became his own residence. Martin and many disciples lived a reproduction of monasticism as known in Egypt, and by the time of Martin's death there were already 2,000 monks in the region. Developments within the Celtic Church of Scotland and Ireland followed monastic patterns in an independent manner, with such an emphasis on solitude and contemplation that monasticism became the norm for missionaries and for the first groups of Christians within an emerging Celtic Christianity.

Monasticism became very popular, particularly after the establishment of Christianity as the 'official religion'.[14] Over the next centuries, monasticism became central to the Church, and monks became revered spiritual heroes, more important than the papacy or the Christian monarchs throughout Europe.[15] Their attempt to reform the Church at different times made them central to the development of Christianity in Europe, and their writing and keeping of manuscripts became a source of learning for the Christian tradition. Monasteries had libraries and *scriptoria*, or writing rooms, where manuscripts were copied. The monks wanted to preserve the Word of God, and at a time when very few people within society could read and write, they were central to the foundation of learning. However, the Benedictine *Lectio Divina*, a continuous daily reading and studying of texts, did not have the acquisition of knowledge as its central purpose, rather the constant communication in prayer with God and the experience of contemplation through the reading of texts.

One of the most influential monastic reformers was St Benedict of Nursia (480–543 CE), who brought some order into the diversity of monastic experiences. Benedict was scandalized by the vice and corruption he encountered in Rome, and started an ascetic life at Subiaco and later Monte Cassino. With some followers, he started a community, and later in his life wrote a rule for the monastic community, which became known as *The Rule of St Benedict*.[16] He was elected abbot of his community for life, and the tradition of abbots and their symbolic representation of Christ's authority over the community started to appear within the Benedictine communities, whereby monks remained within a community for life, under the authority of an abbot. The *Rule* ordered manual and agricultural work, and the monasteries became successful centres of agricultural production. By medieval times, powerful families had incorporated monasteries into their estates for spiritual purposes of sanctification; however, as a result, monasteries and their abbots became part of the power relations of society.

Monastic reforms throughout the years arose out of the search for further ways of becoming detached from the world and worldly affairs, so that monastic reformers were once again individuals who went searching for a more ascetic life, challenging the monastic status quo, and later were followed by others, forming new monastic communities. Thus, before the completion of the first Christian millennium, new developments took place in the Abbey of Cluny in France that embraced other monasteries in a monastic confederation of strict observance that eventually became too powerful for the lords of the land and was criticized for being too large, too communal and too financially established.

Monastic reactions against Cluny first arose in the form of the foundation by St Romuald in 1012 of the Camaldolese, a group of hermits who, while united in the spirit of solitude, lived the Egyptian monastic ideal by remaining in single cells without community life. That monastic foundation was followed by one of the most significant, and the only one that has never been reformed: the Carthusians, founded by St Bruno in 1084, at the Grande Chartreuse near Grenoble. Finally, the third order that differed from the communal life, the study and the liturgical emphasis of the Benedictines was founded in 1098 in Cîteaux, near Dijon, by St Robert of Molesme, and took the name of the Cistercians. The difference between the Cistercian Order and Cluny was that every monastery was autonomous but united within the same rule and way of life, the Abbot of Cîteaux being *primus inter pares*.

The Fourth Lateran Council in 1215 regulated monastic life and the rules of the monastic orders.

The contemplative and political divide

It could be argued that the Reformation in Europe, with in particular its critical look at the possession of land and power by the monasteries, nourished a certain suspicion of monastic communities that was to be influential for centuries to come. For the monasteries lay at the centre of the reformers' critique of a Church that was too powerful in human terms and too preoccupied with political alliances rather than with the Word of God. It was through the consequent divide between reformed and non-reformed that contemplative prayer was associated with Roman Catholicism and Anglicanism, while the truly reformed churches didn't see the need for mediating prayer communities if the Word of God was available to all. The material destruction of abbeys and monasteries expressed a clear popular resentment, fuelled by those who preached reform and caused violence, death and pillage in the name of the Word of God.

It is very striking to live in the town of St Andrews in Fife, an hour north of Edinburgh, where the Benedictine abbey, which had around 200 monks before the Reformation and saw the development of a centre of trade, religion and learning, lies in ruins – a past spoken about and studied within the university itself. One wonders if a reform of the monasteries could have been possible without so much violence and hatred, and what the justification was for a religious reform in which those who adhered to the Word of God, both Protestants and Catholics, killed others and made so many martyrs.

It was during the twentieth century that various traditions within the Church started drawing spiritual strength and support from the Christian contemplative tradition, and ecumenical communities such as Taizé in France showed the way forward using prayer in community, and solitude and silence, as the basis for personal, communal and societal renewal. Taizé was founded by Brother Roger after World War Two as an ecumenical community, retreating from the ashes of conflict and the Shoah in order to find a firm foundation for understanding in post-war Europe. At that time, the flourishing of monastic vocations after two world wars, and the filling of the monasteries with candidates, reiterated once again the fleeing from the world of those who wanted to become closer to God. The founding of monasteries in Asia, Africa and Latin America provided a new beginning for the monastic ideal of solitude and contemplation that has once again caught the imagination and the practice of many Christians in our contemporary world.

Within the Protestant world, developments within Anglicanism built upon the experience of the Anglican Church that in 1842 had founded the Nashotah Community in Wisconsin. By 1990 there were 168 monastic communities of men and women associated with the Anglican Communion. Lutheran monasteries have been founded in the past 40 years in Denmark and Michigan, while an evangelical monastic community exists in Korea bearing the name of Jesus Abbey. In February 2001, the first Methodist monastery for women, St Brigid of Kildare, was founded in Minnesota, marking a full return to the monastic tradition within the contemporary varied traditions of the Church.

Contemplation as a political act

If Luther abolished the monasteries it was because he saw two doctrinal problems with the monastic understanding of his time: to become a monk was understood as the best way to attain salvation, thus denying the possibility of grace for all; and the entry into a monastery was understood as cleansing the monk from all sin, as if it were a second baptism. Instead of reforming the monasteries, Luther abolished them, and through that theological act crushed the possibilities of communities that dedicated their lives to the worship of God and the sanctification of manual work. The fact that a monastic revival throughout the different Christian traditions has taken place since World War Two speaks of the human need to find ways of approaching contemplation and solitude with God more closely and through a vocational commitment for life.

However, one of the central roles of monasteries within the Church has been the support of lay Christians in their search for God and for a deeper spirituality. Retreat centres, liturgical celebrations and the inclusion of lay members attached to monasteries and abbeys as oblates, or members of lay orders, have given strength to lay commitment within the Church, as well as to their work in society and their involvement within the realms of the socio-political. For it is in that engagement between contemplation of God and work for neighbour that most Christians find their place in the world and their vocation to raise families and to be involved in the power of decision through the election of leaders, lobbying for the marginalized and the praise of God in moments of spiritual consolation and political commitment. This daily engagement with the religious and the political sets cooperation between the world religions and the different faith communities at the centre of a civic duty for a common humanity. This has been central to the common understanding reached, for example, by the Dalai Lama and a former Archbishop of Canterbury, Robert Runcie. Thus, in his memoirs the Dalai Lama writes:

> One religious leader with whom I have had several good conversations is the outgoing Archbishop of Canterbury, Dr Robert Runcie . . . We share the view that religion and politics do mix and both agree that it is the clear duty of religion to serve humanity, that it must not ignore reality.[17]

This is a clear message coming from the leader of the Tibetan Buddhists, who spend most of their lives in contemplation but do not perceive their religious activity as totally separated from their political role in society. After all, the Dalai Lama remains spiritual leader of his Buddhist religious order and political leader of all Tibetans, those within the Tibetan region of China and those living in exile. During 2007, that connection between spiritual welfare and socio-political activity became very clear with the peaceful protests against the military leaders of Burma, in which thousands of Buddhist monks took to the streets to defend the democratic rights of the Burmese people and the restoration of democratically elected institutions in Burma. The same kind of protest took place during 2008 in China in the context of human rights abuses in Tibet.

From contemplation to politics

The Christian figures explored within this book have made an impact within contemporary society by showing that prayer, service and a prophetic life arising out of prayer, contemplation and service to others is possible and indeed central to the development of contemporary society. All of them have been recognized by different sectors of society as beacons of hope within a media-dominated world in which shopping and hedonism seem to be the norm and in which those who serve others seem not to exist. It could be that because of this climate of selfishness and consumerism, these figures stand out as fully human and fully Christian, as examples for others, not only by serving their neighbour by gathering material help, as was the case with Mother Teresa, but also by challenging any status quo within nations that decides to order the world not through cooperation but through war and the massive financial implications of developing and sustaining a large machinery of war, violence and destruction.

If their lives seem not to be part of the lives of ordinary Christians then one must reflect once again on the possibility and the mandate to return from daily activities and worries to a conversation with God, so making a full swing from contemplation to politics, and from politics to contemplation, a habitual rhythm of Christian existence. The two processes, the religious and the political, do not remain separate but flow naturally into one another, nourished by the Word and by the communal worship within a particular faith community. For it is the role of Christians within the contemporary public world that will bring further growth to these communities, rather than a negative assessment of the purity of prayer and the sinfulness of the world. The Catholic theologian William T. Cavanaugh has argued that:

> the distinction between politics and religion was not discovered but invented. Before the seventeenth century, politics was associated with the commonwealth in a broad sense, a political and moral order, which included what we would call state and society. The distinction of ecclesial and civil powers in the medieval period was a distinction not of spatial jurisdictions, nor of means, but of ends; the temporal power served the temporary ends of the *civitas terrena*, which was passing away.[18]

The strength of the faith communities in general, and of Christian commitment in particular, offers a necessary avenue for a world that is ordinarily ordered by democratic institutions of wide civil participation. Neither religious fundamentalism nor categories of religious exclusion will create a society that is fully democratic. However, the faith communities and individual Christians need to take part fully in the civic democratic debates that order society, and contribute fully to the goodness of all. That was the spirit of the Latin American churches over the past 30 years, a spirit that made Christianity grow from a secluded worshipping mode of being to a public engagement with all sectors of society. It is that contemplation and political engagement that goes hand in hand, leaving behind a condemnation of the world or a despair that does not reflect the engagement of Jesus of Nazareth and the Christ of faith with the different sectors of society at his time and particularly a daily engagement with the poor and the marginalized.

Chapter 1 explores the contribution to contemplation and politics of the American monk, writer and contemplative Thomas Merton, and his engagement with issues of his time as well as with interfaith issues within a democratic society.

Chapter 2 explores the contribution of the Nicaraguan priest, poet and government minister Ernesto Cardenal, a disciple of Merton, who founded a contemplative community in Nicaragua and later took part in the Nicaraguan revolution and the first Sandinista government that took over the country in 1979.

Chapter 3 outlines the life and contribution of the Jesuit priest, poet and political activist Daniel Berrigan SJ, who throughout his life has managed to upset the US authorities by reminding the public about the ethical and political implications of the gospel in an era of nuclear proliferation and war among nations.

Chapter 4 explores the life of Dr Sheila Cassidy, medical doctor and lay worker in Chile, who underwent the hard test of Christian discipleship and medical–ethical conduct when asked to examine and treat a wounded revolutionary.

Chapter 5 outlines the life and writings of Archbishop Desmond Tutu, who through his public actions helped bring about the condemnation and end of apartheid in South Africa.

Chapter 6 analyses the history of Mother Teresa of Calcutta, the Albanian nun who became a well-known international figure through caring for the terminally ill and those rejected by society in the slums of India. She not only managed to have an international impact but also expanded this work for the poor to many other countries in the world.

What unites all these figures is their deep sense of contemplative prayer and conversations with the Lord. Thus, Chapters 7 and 8 expand some connections between contemplation and politics in the contemporary understanding of the body and the celebration of the Eucharist. Finally, Chapter 9 opens those connections of contemplation and politics to a possible ordering of a daily life of prayer and a daily involvement with society at large, a Christian imperative for contemplating and voting as an expression of Christian involvement within the world of God in contemporary society.

1

Thomas Merton

By the time of his death in Thailand on 10 December 1968, Thomas Merton had become the most important Catholic intellectual in the USA and a revered figure within the peace movement. Despite the fact that he was so active in corresponding with and supporting peace activists and those involved in interfaith dialogue, he was a member of the Order of Cistercians of the Strict Observance (Trappists), and had lived as a contemplative monk at the Abbey of Gethsemani in Kentucky for 27 years.[1] It was from that life of work and contemplation, of which several years were spent as a hermit, that Merton influenced the politics of the USA at the turbulent time of the Vietnam War. He demonstrated the timeless possibilities of a Christian life lived out in contemplation and political action, and broadened by an experience of Asian world religions and politics.

Contemplative and writer

Thomas Merton was born in Prades in France on 31 January 1915, of a New Zealand-born father, Owen Merton, and an American mother, Ruth Jenkins.[2] Both were artists. After meeting at art school in Paris, they married at St Anne's Church in the Soho area of London. Ruth died of stomach cancer when Merton was six years old, while the family was in New Zealand with Owen's parents. It is striking that once Ruth was hospitalized she never saw her children (Tom and John Paul) again – Tom learned of her fate through a letter she wrote telling him she was about to die.[3] After some schooling in France, during the autumn of 1929 Tom was moved to Oakham, a small English public school of about 200 students, in Rutland in Leicestershire.[4] While at Oakham his father came to visit him, but fell ill while returning to London and was discovered to have a brain tumour. He died at the Middlesex Hospital. During the visit, Merton had told his father that he liked the school, which had become a home for him. When the news of his father's death came, Merton felt alone in the world and wrote:

> I sat there in the dark, unhappy room, unable to think, unable to move, with all the innumerable elements of my isolation crowding in upon me from every side: without a home, without a family, without a country, without a father, apparently without any friends, without any interior peace or confidence or light or understanding of my own – without God, too, without God, without heaven, without grace, without anything.[5]

After completing school and a stint at Cambridge University, in 1935 he enrolled at Columbia University. During this time he converted to Catholicism, a process that he described in his autobiography, *The Seven Storey Mountain*, a book that has sold more than one million copies since its initial publication.[6] His own conversion to Catholicism and to the practice of Christianity was nourished by a strong and close group of friends at Columbia, who remained close to Merton for the rest of his life. The atmosphere at Columbia was charged with the possibility of connecting academic institutions with ordinary lives, and before World War Two there were a number of active Communist students as well as a very strong anti-war movement connected to other European universities such as Oxford.[7] Monica Furlong comments that:

> like the students at Oxford who were, at the same time, vowing that in the event of war they would not fight for 'king and country', because they felt all war was wrong, the students at Columbia stoutly proclaimed in a massive demonstration in the gym that they would not fight under any circumstances.[8]

In 1938, Merton, having completed his degree, enrolled in the graduate school of English and started work on a thesis entitled 'Nature and Art in William Blake', and began to feel that he wanted to become a university teacher. It was through reading for his thesis, particularly Thomas Aquinas and Jacques Maritain, that Merton realized that some of his naturalistic premises didn't make sense – up to then, he had given little thought to the possibility that human beings related to a natural as well as to a supernatural world in their lives.[9] He attended a low Mass and was enchanted by the atmosphere in the congregation, and read Catholic theological books, through which he realized that unlike his childhood experience, the practice of Catholicism was deeply reflexive, to the extent that rationalism and academic discussions enriched the faith rather than impeded it. On 16 November 1938 he was baptized and received Holy Communion, accompanied by his friends from Columbia University.

By then Merton had become a very serious Catholic and his consideration of becoming a priest came through prayer, and while in adoration of the Blessed Sacrament. It was Dan Walsh, a lay lecturer in philosophy and one of Merton's teachers, who helped him sort out the options among religious congregations and religious orders. Walsh had been to Gethsemani for a retreat and alerted Merton to the possibilities of the spiritual life and the happiness of many who had joined a religious order. Merton's decision was to become a Franciscan, and he applied but was initially rejected. It was now the end of 1940, and the Japanese attack on Pearl Harbor triggered a certain anxiety in Merton to try his religious vocation before being drafted into the US Army; he decided to do so at Gethsemani – the Franciscans, who had now decided to accept him into their novitiate, were kept waiting. During the previous Easter Merton had spent some days at Gethsemani and had loved the experience, particularly of simplicity, as described in his autobiography:

They were poor, they had nothing, and therefore they were free and possessed everything, and everything they touched struck off something of the fire of divinity. And they worked with their hands, silently ploughing and harrowing the earth, and sowing seed in obscurity, and reaping their small harvests to feed themselves and the other poor.[10]

Merton wrote to the US Army requesting a postponement to his drafting, and was given a month to sort out his situation.[11] After asking to join the monastery as soon as possible, he gave away his possessions, burnt the manuscripts of a couple of novels he had been working on and took the train to Kentucky. After a short spell at the Guest House, together with another arrival, Merton was admitted to the novitiate by the Abbot and in a moment left the outside world and became one of those aspiring to become Trappists. Merton wrote:

> at the other end of the long dark hall we went into a room where three monks were sitting at typewriters, and we handed over our fountain pens and wristwatches and our loose cash to the Treasurer, and signed documents promising that if we left the monastery we would not sue the monks for back wages for hours of manual labour.[12]

On 10 December 1941 he entered the community at the Abbey of Gethsemani, thus joining the strictest monastic order of the Catholic Church: 'the life in a Trappist monastery was self-consciously rigorous and penitential. The diet was vegetarian, with meat provided only for the elderly or the sick.'[13] The daily prayer life was intense and was necessarily so, as already pointed to in an entry in Merton's 1941 diary written while visiting Gethsemani:

> The life in this abbey is not understandable unless you begin the day with the monks, with Matins at 2 a.m. . . . . The hours from 2 to 8 (6 hours) are all devoted to prayer, and all pretty much filled up with prayer, by the time Matins, Lauds, Prime and all the little hours (at least in Lent) are said.[14]

Merton's choice was striking because intellectuals and writers tended to join the Benedictines, where prayer and study went together, while the Trappists stressed manual and communal farm work. However, Merton managed to feel at home outside the world that had captivated him before, and while he thought many times throughout his life about moving to another monastery, he never mentioned the possibility of not being a contemplative monk.[15] As a result, his own search for a more meaningful monastic life evolved from that of a medieval recluse to one of a writer, always deluged with hundreds of letters and requests, and always happy to return to his hours of solitude, contemplation and study.

Contemplative writing as politics

Even as he entered the contemplative life at Gethsemani, Merton the writer and poet never quit his habit of keeping a personal diary, which had already begun while he was at school. His beginnings as an aspirant Trappist were recorded in *The Sign of Jonas*, a collection of his diaries from 1946 to 1952 that reflects his adjustment to community life, even to sleep in a dormitory, within the climate of the post-war USA, in which vocations increased dramatically after the personal nightmares suffered by US personnel in the campaigns of Europe and the South Pacific.[16] During that period Merton wrote of conversations with his Lord, and his leitmotiv is eternity and his personal search for eternity. Thus, contemplation as a way of life remains a personal quest for holiness in a secluded atmosphere away from the worldly preoccupations of most Christians. Merton writes:

> there is greater comfort in the substance of silence than in the answer to a question. Eternity is in the present. Eternity is in the palm of the hand. Eternity is a seed of fire, whose sudden roots break barriers that keep my heart from being an abyss.[17]

Later meditations and writings, starting in 1956, on more contemporary issues were summarized in the volume *Conjectures of a Guilty Bystander*.[18]

Merton searched for further solitude after taking his final vows as a Cistercian monk in 1947, and his priestly ordination on Ascension Thursday in 1949. However, the Abbot asked him to become master of scholastics in 1951, in charge of those monks who were preparing for their final profession. It was a role that Merton fulfilled until 1955, when he became master of novices. By the late 1950s Merton was already unhappy about the fact that because of the service to the new monks he had little time to pray and contemplate; however, he fulfilled all the community prayer times, took part in the community manual work and prepared conferences and talks for the scholastics and the novices that clearly required lots of preparation and were mostly of publishable quality. Indeed, between 1952 and 1960 Merton wrote ten books as well as many pamphlets and essays. In his reading, study and writing on a wide variety of topics, he always asked the same intellectual question vis-à-vis his life as a contemplative monk: 'How can a contemplative monk in the twentieth century not be concerned with these issues?'[19] These topics were numerous and his discussion of them, as the tapes of his conferences show, was inspiring; there were few monks at the time who would have dreamed of amassing such a volume of knowledge on so many subjects and achieving such clarity in their writing.

The quantity of his writing on religious, philosophical and journalistic issues was enormous, numbering thousands of items.[20] His years as a novice master allowed him to come into contact with devout novices from many different countries. One of these was Ernesto Cardenal, the Nicaraguan poet and later member of the Sandinista government, who was at Gethsemani for two years but was advised to leave because of ill-health (see Chapter 2). It was the experience of being a novice master that allowed him to become more attuned to the concerns of the world, in that he listened to the experiences and aspirations of his own novices who had left the world not so long ago. However, it was his intellectual capacity for enquiry and for reading and studying that brought him into an ongoing dialogue with many religious practitioners over concerns about the practice of religion within the USA of the 1960s. This period coincided with two major events: the US involvement in

Vietnam and the advent of a period of renewal by the Catholic Church through the Second Vatican Council (1962–5).

The latter coincided with Merton's search for a place of his own, a hermitage in which he could live and pray, only occasionally taking meals with the rest of the Trappist community. The idea had come about by the late 1950s and coincided with the visit of a monk from Cuernavaca in Mexico, who suggested to Merton that he might leave Gethsemani and join a monastery outside the USA. Merton requested permission from his Abbot, who had to write to Rome because of the vow of stability taken by every contemplative monk, but his request was finally denied.[21] However, the hermitage and retreat centre within the premises of Gethsemani allowed Merton independence and solitude in order to continue writing in a place where he could receive some of his visitors and where some ecumenical meetings were held.[22] By this time he had been living temporarily outside the sleeping quarters of Gethsemani for a couple of years, and finally in August 1965 he moved to the newly furnished hermitage, with the official permission of the abbey's private council.[23] After his first five days of complete solitude Merton wrote: 'Over and over again I see that this life is what I have always hoped it would be and always sought. A life of peace, silence, purpose, meaning.'[24]

Merton enjoyed his solitude at the hermitage and was able to structure his reading and writing around the praying of the hours and other hours of contemplation during the day. A keen photographer and lover of nature, he describes in his diaries his awe for the changes of the seasons, birds, storms, snow and so on.[25] Somehow, Merton enjoyed the possibility of going out for a meal with some of his visitors, and was able to cope with successive minor ailments and back problems that involved hospital treatment. It is surprising that despite the changes in his monastic routine, Merton remained ever the contemplative, assessing every event in terms of God's involvement with his own person and with the world around. His acquired freedom brought a short emotional involvement with a young woman, but even through that crisis Merton continued to view his contemplative way of life as the one where he was happiest, even when he longed for the possibility of living it in another monastery, a quieter one with new surroundings.[26] A year after he had moved to the hermitage Merton made a written promise, witnessed by the Abbot, in which he stated that after a year's probation he promised to spend the rest of his life in solitude 'in so far as my health may permit'.[27]

However, Merton's influence on his contemporary political situation was enormous. He was well known through his writings, and as a Catholic best-selling author had an influence on many other Catholics within the USA. By the 1960s, and with the conflict in Vietnam at heart, Merton exchanged correspondence with the Jesuit Daniel Berrigan and others who objected to war and who were exercising peaceful protest against the drafting of young Americans into the US military (see Chapter 3). Daniel Berrigan visited Merton at Gethsemani in 1962, and years later Merton wrote to friends about his middle way between the shock techniques of the Berrigan brothers (Daniel and Philip) and the views of those who supported war as a Christian duty to the state, and some Catholic bishops who spoke of the Vietnam War as an act of Christian love.[28] His position regarding war and violence was very clear, as expressed in midsummer 1968 in a circular letter to friends:

> I am against war, against violence, against violent revolution, for peaceful settlement of differences, for non-violent but nevertheless radical change. Change is needed, and violence will not really change anything: at most it will only transfer power from one set of bull-headed authorities to another . . .[29]

However, he objected to the refusal to grant permission for the Berrigan brothers' book against the war to be published.[30] Over the years Merton became quite fond of Daniel Berrigan and his stand for gospel values, while Berrigan in turn considered him a teacher and a friend.[31] Merton's civil position vis-à-vis the draft was that of someone who had escaped conscription because of his monastic life; he was not prepared to confront the military authorities in the manner that the Berrigan brothers had, by burning draft cards and spilling blood on files after breaking into federal administrative centres for conscription.[32] But no other contemplative in the history of the USA has had more influence on political activity than Merton, even though some American Catholics distrusted his ideas on the Vietnam War and, further, started to distrust his growing engagement with the religious traditions of Asia, particularly Buddhism.

Merton's contemplative writings included his usual talks within the monastery but extended beyond the genre of the contemporary and political. His literary excellence meant that he kept a group of literary friends with whom he corresponded extensively and who recognized Merton as a writer, though for Merton the division was artificial – all his literary writings, including his poetry, came out of his monastic experience and his personal contemplative life. Among his literary friends were Ernesto Cardenal, his former novice and Nicaraguan poet, Evelyn Waugh, Jacques Maritain, the Chilean poet Nicanor Parra, the Venezuelan poet Ludovico Silva and the Argentinian writer Victoria Ocampo.[33] Merton's interest in Latin America and its writers remained one of his most fruitful because, unlike his other friends, what Merton shared with them was literature itself rather than faith or religion. Nicanor Parra, for example, was an atheist and part of one of the most prominent Communist families of Chile; however, unlike his relatives, Nicanor followed not an artistic career but an academic one, having studied mathematics, physics and cosmology at Brown University and the University of Oxford and having later become a professor of theoretical physics. Together with the publisher and poet James Laughlin, Parra visited Merton in May 1966, and Merton wrote to him before exchanging poems and suggestions. Later, Merton wrote a warm letter to Parra on the occasion of his sister's suicide: 'I am very sorry, and wish I could say something that might help you in your sorrow. But there are occasions when words are no help. In my friendship I think of you and share your sorrow.'[34]

But it was towards the East that Merton was looking, both in order to understand other faiths and to consolidate his reading of Asian religions that had been encouraged by the Japanese scholar Daisetz Teitaro Suzuki (1870–1966), who had through many lectures interpreted Zen Buddhism to the West and Christianity to the East. Merton met Suzuki in New York in 1964 and they corresponded frequently about details of Zen that were to prove central to Merton's trip to Asia in 1968.

Christianity and Buddhism

Merton's trip to Asia came about due to an invitation extended by a Benedictine group that was helping the possible implementation of renewal throughout the world as required by the Second Vatican Council. The idea was to gather in a conference all Asian monastic leaders, including Benedictines and Cistercians, in Bangkok (Thailand) in December 1968. Merton also agreed to give an address to the Spiritual Summit Conference in Calcutta and to give a series of talks at different monasteries in Asia. However, he wanted to visit as many Buddhist monasteries as possible; according to his secretary, Brother Patrick Hart, 'Thomas Merton's pilgrimage to Asia was an effort on his part to deepen his own religious and monastic commitment.'[35]

Merton had a sustained interest in Asian monasticism and had read extensively on Zen and Buddhism in general.[36] Had he not died in December 1968, it is arguable that he would have done groundbreaking work in interfaith Christian–Buddhist relations. Merton's Asian trip was authorized by his Abbot so that he might report back on the possibilities of Cistercian expansion in Asia, this despite the fact that his Abbot had little confidence in Merton's practical abilities as a decision-maker. Previously Merton had explored the possibilities of founding monastic communities in Alaska but, because he had visited during summer, had missed the fact that due to bad weather and fog, visibility during winter was nil.

Throughout his Asian visit, Merton kept a diary that was later published.[37] It is striking, throughout his diary, how conversant Merton was with Buddhist and Sanskrit terminology and how all his conversations related to monastic issues and his search for further solitude. Thus, after days of visiting places and people he could think only that he needed a few days of solitude, and it was perhaps because of this that his visit to Dharamsala (India), where the headquarters of the Tibetan government in exile and the sacred places associated with the Fourteenth Dalai Lama are still located, became one of the highlights of his trip (along with the conferences he gave to other Cistercians and Benedictines).[38]

Merton and the Dalai Lama met three times during November 1968.[39] Their first meeting, on 4 November, dealt with religion and philosophy and ways of meditating, and Merton listened attentively to what he had to say about Tibetan Buddhism, which was criticized by other more traditional Buddhist schools of thought and practice.[40] Their second meeting took place on 6 November, when they discussed epistemology and the mind, particularly Tibetan and Western–Thomist theories.[41] Later, they discussed meditation, and the Dalai Lama showed Merton the essential position for meditation whereby 'the right hand (discipline) is above the left (wisdom)'; in Zen it is the other way around.[42] Merton commented on the Dalai Lama's way of thinking as follows: 'I like the solidity of the Dalai Lama's ideas. He is a very consecutive thinker and moves from step to step. His ideas of the interior life are built on very solid foundations and on a real awareness of practical problems.'[43] Their third meeting took place on 8 November, when they discussed Western monastic life, vows and dietary prohibitions, among other things.[44] Merton raised the point of monasticism and Marxism, the topic of his Bangkok lecture, and the Dalai Lama, who admired Marxism, suggested that 'from a certain point of view it was impossible for monks and Communists to get along, but that perhaps it should not be entirely impossible *if* Marxism meant *only* the establishment of an equitable economic and social structure'.[45] By the end of the visit there had formed between them a natural closeness and a spiritual bond; later the Dalai Lama recognized that Merton's death had deprived the world of the possibility of a meaningful dialogue between Christians and Buddhists with all their similarities.[46]

During his Asian trip Merton delivered a lecture on 'Marxism and monastic perspectives', a clear sign of the direction of his thinking on contemplation and politics at a time when the Cold War had triggered a distrust of Marxism in the USA and a distrust of religion in the USSR, China and Eastern Europe.[47] In his lecture Merton relies on the thought of the philosopher Herbert Marcuse, whom he considered 'as a kind of monastic thinker'.[48] Indeed, for Merton Marxism's task of removing unnecessary oppressive structures coincided with the need for removal of what impedes a monastic openness to the divine through the opening and the grounding of the subconscious. Merton's use of the thought of Ludwig Feuerbach points to a materialistic reality – in Feuerbach's words, 'Man is what he eats'.[49] In simple terms, the Marxist looks at human beings where they are and assesses the possibility of change; the contemplative does the same, for the monasteries have always been places where those in need go for food and shelter. Merton makes a clear distinction between materialism and contemplation, but argues that both projects create a challenge to the structures of society and state clearly that society needs change and that human beings are not at the centre of the aims and objectives of structures within society. At the end the monk remains apart from the world not so as to avoid it but to transform it so that 'the monk belongs to the world, but the world belongs to him insofar as he has dedicated himself totally to liberation from it in order to liberate it'.[50] At the end of the lecture Merton assured his audience that he would be following the discussion in the evening, and pronounced his last words: 'So I will disappear.'[51] And so he did: as he prepared himself for a siesta in his room, an electric fan fell on him and he died due to a heart attack.[52]

After his sudden exit from the world, Merton's contemplative life and influence on contemporary politics became an agenda for others. There is no doubt that his monastic experience of Christianity influenced the politics of the 1960s. His writings, too, continued to influence those who carried on with a life of contemplation and politics and who had had personal contact with him – such as Ernesto Cardenal and Daniel Berrigan, the subjects of the next two chapters.

2

Ernesto Cardenal

The Nicaraguan priest, poet and contemplative Ernesto Cardenal became the centre of attention of the world media when Pope John Paul II visited Nicaragua in 1983. John Paul II had been in office for just a year when the Sandinista revolution took over the government in Nicaragua in 1979, as a result of which the Vatican had to deal with the involvement of three priests in active roles within Nicaraguan politics: Ernesto Cardenal as Minister for Culture, Fernando Cardenal SJ as National Youth Coordinator and Miguel D'Scoto as Foreign Minister.[1] Their political commitment was questioned by John Paul II when he visited Nicaragua in 1983, but Cardenal stated clearly that as a monk and a priest he saw his role as minister as a sacrifice of love for others. However, if the Vatican started a theological questioning of the liberation theologians in private, in public and on arrival in Managua for his papal visit, John Paul II wagged his finger at Ernesto Cardenal, who was at the airport among the ministers of the revolutionary government. Cardenal interpreted this as 'a humiliating gesture' of annoyance by John Paul II that there was a Latin American revolution that didn't persecute the Church, in which Christians and Marxists, including priests, worked together for the good of society, and that 'the theology of liberation was in power'.[2]

However, all that Cardenal ever did in politics, revolution and social involvement was framed and triggered by his contemplative life, in which his love for God and his desire to see God's face brought him to the Abbey of Gethsemani in Kentucky. He stayed for two years, before being advised to leave that contemplative life because of ill-health. During that time

Merton was Cardenal's novice master and a strong influence on his development within his life of contemplation and politics.

From Nicaragua to Gethsemani

Cardenal was born in Granada, Nicaragua, on 20 January 1925, into one of the first Spanish families to have arrived from Europe in the twentieth century, as the son of Rodolfo and Esmeralda (Martínez) Cardenal.[3] When he was five years old the family moved to the town of León, where Rubén Darío, the greatest Nicaraguan poet, had been born. Ernesto was educated in a Catholic school run by the Christian Brothers until he was ten years old, when his parents sent him to Centroamérica, the Jesuit boarding school in Granada. The school had close contact with two renowned poets, José Coronel Urtecho and Pablo Antonio Cuadra. Cardenal was related to both, and his grandmother encouraged him to read poetry at all times. At the school the Spanish Jesuit and poet Angel Martínez Baigorri also guided him and encouraged him to write poetry. It is said that his love for a young lady, Carmen, triggered a vast number of his early poems; however, the main influences on his early poetry were in fact Pablo Neruda and César Vallejo.[4]

After completing secondary school, Cardenal studied philosophy and letters at the University of Mexico (1942–6) and English literature at Columbia University (1947–9). It was in New York, while at Columbia, that Cardenal was influenced by Ezra Pound, and where he read for the first time the poems of Thomas Merton.[5] It was by reading and studying American poetry and Pound's direct treatment of the subject, without using any superfluous words, that Cardenal found his vein of direct and revolutionary poetry.[6] And it was by reading Merton, and through his own life with Merton, that Cardenal made poverty a sine qua non for the act of poetry and the life of a poet. After a few months in Madrid and Paris, in 1950 he returned to Nicaragua and became an active member of the revolutionary group UNAP (National Union for Popular Action). In 1952 he had to go into hiding because of his political activities, and he took part in the failed plot against President Somoza in 1954. UNAP had planned to surprise Somoza inside his palace and take over power. The plan collapsed because the plotters were too few in number, and most were arrested after one of Cardenal's comrades, under torture, gave information to the security forces. Cardenal's hiding is mentioned in his poem 'Hora 0'.[7]

In 1956, when the poet Rigoberto López Pérez assassinated Somoza, Cardenal underwent a religious conversion and applied to become a Trappist monk in the USA. On 8 May 1957 he entered the Trappist monastery of Gethsemani and started his novitiate under Thomas Merton, who was then novice master.[8] Cardenal had to sign an agreement with the Abbot stating that he would not write poetry or at least not have it published, and he took a new name, Mary Lawrence (as Mary is the order's patroness, all Trappist monks take the name Mary as their first name).[9] His love for God and the renunciation of the life he loved made him join the austerity of Gethsemani, thus rejecting the possibility either of being a priest in Nicaragua or of enjoying the country's natural beauty, which was very dear to him.[10] In his memoirs Cardenal recalls how, when he arrived in the USA, the immigration officer reminded him that the only way he could be admitted was by immigrating for life, and welcomed him to a new country, a new life and a commitment to live in Gethsemani for the rest of his life.[11] As outlined in Chapter 1, Gethsemani was one of the most austere monastic enclaves of the Catholic Church, and before the reforms of Vatican II even more austere than today, when monks have their own individual rooms and freedom to correspond with the outside world. At that time, and in the description provided by Jim Forest:

> The monks slept in their robes on straw-covered boards in dormitories that were frigid in winter and sweltering in summer. Beds were separated by shoulder-high partitions. Half the year was fasting time. A typical meal featured bread, potatoes, an apple and barley coffee. Even on such feast days as Easter and Christmas, meat, fish and eggs were never served.[12]

During the first days at Gethsemani Cardenal had a mentor who guided him and taught him, among other things, a hand language, totally silent, that had been developed by the Trappists during the twelfth century.[13] The sign language was useful in the Trappist life of complete silence, but even then could not be used between 7 p.m. and 7 a.m., the period of the so-called Great Silence. Cardenal remembers that the novices did not join the community for morning office or Mass but had Mass with Merton, who later during the day would work sowing tomato seeds, for example, together with the novices. During the daily life there were no breaks in between prayer, study, manual work or meals, so that for Cardenal that life was 'a life of love' without holidays.[14]

Shortly after Cardenal's arrival, Merton mentioned to him the idea of setting up a monastic Trappist foundation from Gethsemani in Nicaragua, and over the following decades both of them would write to each other about the possibilities.[15] However, Merton, who wanted to move to Latin America, was never allowed to join the Trappist pioneers who established a new monastery in Santiago, Chile. Even the Abbot was learning Spanish in case they needed him in Latin America, as the monasteries in the USA were filling very quickly – at that time there were almost one thousand Trappist monks in the USA. Because of the possibility of a foundation in Nicaragua, and Cardenal's literary past, Merton asked him to check the Spanish translation of *The Seven Storey Mountain* that had been commissioned by Editorial Sudamericana.[16] Merton was also honest with Cardenal about his criticisms of what he started to call the Trappist Corporation – comments that unsettled Cardenal, who was, at that time, very happy at Gethsemani and wanted to continue growing in his practice of the monastic life.[17]

Parts of Cardenal's memoirs are concerned with the daily community meeting, the chapter, in which deceased Trappists were remembered and where a monk read a chapter of the *Rule of St Benedict*.[18] Other than a chapter of faults, in which monks asked pardon from the community for their trespasses, there were few occasions on which the whole community gathered together in one place. During the chapter of faults one monk was singled out by the Abbot and had to confess a particular fault; in the case of Cardenal, he always asked pardon for being late, while he was accused by others of being noisy when closing doors and of speaking loudly to a visitor (Pablo Antonio Cuadra).[19] At that time there were almost 200 people in Gethsemani, so that it was a large community that gathered to listen to the *Rule* and encourage each other to continue the life of John the Baptist in the desert, as Merton used to tell the novices.

One of the problems faced by Cardenal was his inability to sing and chant the office in chapel. Despite having several teachers he was unable to appreciate the different tones, and Merton told him that such a lack was an impediment for priestly ordination because the priest needed to lead the singing during the High Mass.[20] However, the Abbot thought that this would not be a problem as within the new Latin American foundation there would probably be other liturgical practices. It was during this discussion that Cardenal expressed his opinion that his call was to a contemplative life rather than to the Catholic priesthood, and that he would be happy to remain as a non-ordained Trappist within Gethsemani. This was important because it would give meaning to all of Cardenal's life, in which contemplation took precedence over the priesthood and over his ministerial duties in government (even when as Minister of Culture in the Sandinista government Cardenal had to attend musical events, he immersed himself in prayer, as he wasn't able to discern the quality of the music being played in front of him).

It was Merton who introduced Cardenal to the value of the indigenous thought and spirituality of North and South America, and who insisted that the Latin American monastery to be opened should have indigenous monks as well as those from North America. The impact on Cardenal's poetry and writing was enormous – the indigenous and pre-Colombian peoples and their myths started filling his poetry after he left

Gethsemani.[21] Cardenal had a constant headache and stomach-ache during his last few months in Gethsemani. The monk-doctor suggested that the gastritis was caused by nervous tension and that this created the headache because Cardenal recognized that once the bell for the office in chapel rang he started feeling ill. The doctor suggested that the problem would only be solved by leaving Gethsemani and joining another, less strict, contemplative community, such as the Benedictines.[22] It was decided that Cardenal should leave Gethsemani, and while the decision was taken Merton introduced him to Dom Gregorio Lemercier, the Belgian-born Prior of the Benedictine monastery of St Mary in Cuernavaca, Mexico, who welcomed him.[23] Thus, at the end of July 1950, Cardenal left Gethsemani with Merton's clear instructions to wait for him in Cuernavaca, as Merton too was applying to leave Gethsemani.[24] As Cardenal met Merton for the last time he knelt in front of him request-ing his blessing; years later, in October 1965, when Cardenal was already a priest and visited Merton in order to discuss the new contemplative community in the archipelago of Solentiname, it was Merton who knelt in front of Cardenal to receive his blessing.[25]

Contemplative life in Solentiname

From Gethsemani Cardenal went to Mexico City and then to Cuernavaca, where he conveyed messages from Merton to Lemercier regarding Merton's request to leave Gethsemani. This needed to be assessed by his spiritual director, the later Cardinal of Paris, Jean Daniélou, who could not agree with Merton's changing his vow of stability as a Trappist for another experimental way of contemplative life.[26] However, neither Cardenal nor Merton knew this at the time, and Cardenal proceeded to follow Merton's instructions, arriving as a guest at the Benedictine monastery of Cuernavaca, Santa María de la Resurrección. Cuernavaca was ahead of its time. Already at the time of Cardenal's arrival the liturgy was sung in Spanish rather than Latin, and the church was filled with beautiful contemporary icons. Lemercier placed a heavy emphasis on psychoanalytical techniques and group therapy related to the religious life and contemplation. In 1962 the Vatican ordered that he cease using these techniques, which resulted in his leaving the religious life and getting married, a fact that saddened Merton because the new way of being contemplative tried in Cuernavaca had been lost for ever.[27]

Cardenal was 34 years old and his first two books, *Epigramas* and *Hora 0*, had just been published. He had few possessions while a guest at the monastery, and continued corresponding with Merton, who was still hopeful of leaving Gethsemani for Cuernavaca.[28] Merton's Abbot was suspicious, and the letters were marked 'conscience matter', indicating absolute privacy from the Abbot's censorship. However, at the end of the year Merton wrote to Dom Lemercier and to Cardenal, informing them that he had received a letter from Rome rejecting his request to leave Gethsemani and ordering him not to pursue the matter any further.[29] At the same time Merton offered to continue as novice master due to the fact that he had the possibility of some personal solitude, and was 'better off here than at any other time in the monastery'.[30] Further, he supported Cardenal's efforts in Nicaragua and accepted the will of the Sacred Congregation as God's will for him.[31] Merton seemed to move on very quickly, and asked Jean Daniélou to continue supporting him as spiritual director.[32]

In the meantime Cardenal began his studies for the priesthood at the Cuernavaca monastery, but still as a guest. By the end of 1961 he had left for a seminary in Colombia and restarted his correspondence with Merton.[33] He moved to La Ceja in Colombia in order to continue his studies for the priesthood, and remained 'from 1961 to 1965'. It was at La Ceja that Cardenal wrote his own rephrased version of the psalms, *Salmos*. Because of its revolutionary reading of the Hebrew Scriptures, *Salmos* was translated into many languages, and was considered subversive by the police in several Latin American countries.[34] It was through *Salmos* that Cardenal became a well-known Latin American poet.[35] On completing his theological studies he was ordained as a Catholic priest at the Colegio de la Asunción in Managua on 15 August 1965.

After his ordination Cardenal was not sent to a parish but started a priestly life that was to be rather different from that of other priests. The thought of starting a Trappist foundation in Nicaragua was still in Cardenal's mind, and he continued to be enchanted with the idea of a simple and contemplative life closer to the original life of the Trappists.[36] As Merton could not join him, Cardenal moved to the islands of Solentiname, together with two former Colombian classmates, Carlos Alberto and William Agudelo.[37] Two poets, Pablo Antonio Cuadra and José Coronel Urtecho, accompanied them on their journey.[38] Three of them started their community life on 13 February 1966.

The Colombians did not stay long. Carlos Alberto found that a monastic life did not suit him, while William Agudelo missed his Colombian girlfriend, Teresita. They both left but eventually Agudelo and Teresita rejoined the monastic community that, after consultation with Merton, had been expanded to include married people. The community followed the traditional search for God through the recognition that contemplation led to him. It is interesting that Cardenal recognized that he went to Solentiname searching for God in contemplation and found a God who eventually led him to others, to revolution and to Marxism as a tool for social change. It was the reading of the gospel that led him to Marxism; it was contemplation that led him to revolution.[39]

Cardenal identified his community with a lay monastery under the name of Our Lady of Solentiname. William Agudelo and Teresita had two children named Irene and Juan, and they were joined by some local young men, Alejandro, Elbis and Laureano. They cultivated and lived on the produce of the land, while from the start they also produced objects that could be sold, and which later were sold all over the world. These included ashtrays, candlesticks and souvenirs in the shape of local fauna. They shared their profits in a common purse from which the needs of each individual community member were supplied. The utopian nature of the community was summarized by Cardenal's wish that one day there would be no money in the world and that everybody would be filled with love for each other.

When the monastic experiment ended because of the bombardment of the islands by Somoza's armed forces, some of the transcripts of those conversations that took place after the reading of the Gospel at the Sunday Mass became important testimonies to Cardenal's creativity, and to the driving force of contemplation in the life of a priest who became identified with the politics of the Nicaraguan revolution and with the involvement of Latin American priests in politics. However, as Cardenal expressed it during the moments in which he found the life of a government minister tough, he was only interrupting his contemplative life in order to serve the people; he was looking forward to the day when he would cease to be a politician.

In a short introduction to the two volumes of *The Gospel in Solentiname*, Cardenal explained the *Sitz im Leben* of these commentaries, collated and published in Europe.[40] He stressed that there were different personalities involved in the commentaries, which ultimately were the work of the Spirit within an archipelago in which not everybody had access to a boat so as to reach Cardenal's community, and within a Eucharistic celebration in which copies of the New Testament were distributed to all participants, but some of whom, particularly the elderly, could not read.[41] After the Mass all participants shared a simple but communal lunch.

The communal commentary spoke of the involvement of Christians within Nicaraguan society, in which social injustice and oppression by landowners was ordinary reality. Take, for example, the passage from Matthew 22.15–22, where Jesus is challenged on his allegiance to Caesar and/or God, and in which at the end he tells those present, 'Give to Caesar what is Caesar's and to God what is God's'.[42] Cardenal commented that those questions were designed to trap Jesus, to see what he would say. Laureano commented that Jesus told them to build the Kingdom of love and to wait for a confrontation with Rome that would only take place later; in other words, the emperor loved his image on the coins and what Jesus was asking his disciples was to love God first and not the selfishness of money.[43] Alejandro expanded the idea by reminding the group that at that time the emperor was considered God and Jesus was challenging the possibility of paying taxes to a foreign ruler who was neither the God of the Jews nor the God that Jesus was speaking about; Jesus was speaking against Roman imperialism and he speaks against all imperialism today.[44] Cardenal linked the different comments in one long conversation, and after Alejandro had spoken argued that Jesus was acting like a politician, as a leader of the people who does not change his opinion because he is pushed to do so; Jesus not only spoke to the Jews about the politics of that time but he speaks to all peoples now as well. For Cardenal, there is still imperialism today associated with service to money; however, for him, to give to God what is God's is to take part in a revolution. Indeed, for Cardenal, God liberates because he is always pushing for change, for a revolution – that is the message of all prophets.[45] All those present agreed that money in itself was good but that selfishness because of money was not.

Many visitors arrived at Solentiname to see for themselves what was happening in that contemplative community, and on one occasion Brother Juan, an American, was among them. He was dressed in a white robe, lived very simply (even though his parents were hoteliers in South Africa) and his belongings were minimal: only one robe, a change of underwear, a copy of the Gospels and a flute. He spoke Spanish very well and told those present that he was going from place to place as a disciple of Jesus and as a follower of Saint Francis of Assisi. In sharing about his life with those who were at the Sunday Eucharist, he told them that he had decided not to use money, relying rather on the help of people to go from place to place, to eat and have somewhere to sleep. While in Colombia he had met another American pilgrim, who told him about Solentiname, and he had decided to visit Cardenal's community on his way to India, living the life of a mendicant similar to that of the medieval orders. Cardenal commented that they never heard of him again; he told them that he didn't write letters.[46]

Poetry as contemplation

With the arrival of Cardenal on the largest island of Mancarrón in 1966, the remote and deprived area of the archipelago of Solentiname came to develop a strong sense of community. Solentiname is completely isolated from the rest of Nicaragua and the closest town, San Carlos, is one hour away by boat. San Carlos is a further hour by boat across Lake Nicaragua from any of the other Nicaraguan trading centres. Those living around the archipelago were poor peasants who managed to bring their products, mainly beans, rice and fish, to San Carlos, and were paid very little; thus they remained in poverty without any hope of getting out of it. The only visitors were politicians who wanted their votes or local priests who before Cardenal's arrival told them to love God and remain where they were.

Cardenal's arrival presented them with preaching that was rather different, and he gave them some cohesion in their aspirations for a better and more just society. At the same time they managed to organize themselves, opening a school, a library and a museum, while Solentiname had a large workshop where local artisans started to work. Later, with encouragement from Cardenal, some local artists started painting, and their output was exported to markets in North America and Europe, bringing not only international recognition and dignity but also much needed income to the community and to the projects that allowed peasant families to have food and shelter. However, among those flourishing groups of craftsmen and painters there were no poets. As the Costa Rican poet Mayra Jiménez remarked in 1976, this was strange, as Cardenal was a very accomplished poet. Cardenal invited Jiménez to visit

Solentiname and to lead some poetry workshops, and she arrived in November 1976. After the Sunday Mass she spoke to those who had shown interest – a group of 30 or so – and realized that they did not know that Cardenal was a poet; however, they wrote poetry very easily and naturally and reacted with enormous enthusiasm when Cardenal's was read.[47] A collection of their poetry was published by the Nicaraguan Ministry of Culture after the triumph of the Nicaraguan revolution, and a shorter English translation also became available.[48]

By 1976 Cardenal was already fully involved with the *Frente Sandinista de Liberación Nacional* (FSLN), and on its behalf attended the meetings of the Russell Tribunal in Rome that discussed human rights violations in Nicaragua and the whole of Latin America. On 13 October 1977, young people staying at the community of Solentiname decided to join the FSLN and took part in the armed attack against the San Carlos barracks, where Somoza's National Guard for Solentiname was stationed.[49] Immediately after that attack the National Guard took over the island and destroyed buildings and infrastructure. Along with others, Cardenal sought refuge in Costa Rica and was condemned in his absence to many years in prison. He wrote a moving letter to the people of Nicaragua explaining the genesis and aims of the Solentiname community, that they sought contemplation and a closer union with God and that through contemplation they had made a political commitment to a non-violent revolution. Later, however, they had realized that an armed revolution was needed, and joined that process. Cardenal included himself in those community developments; however, he was always a non-violent revolutionary who admitted that reading the Gospels had made him that way. Solentiname existed for 12 years, and the islands suffered intense repression and violence throughout 1978 while Cardenal remained in exile in Costa Rica. During those years in exile, he represented the FSLN at international meetings and visited many countries seeking international solidarity for its cause. However, once the Sandinista forces gained ground against Somoza and eventually defeated him, Cardenal returned to Managua and joined the Sandinista government as minister for culture.

Cardenal the poet, Cardenal the politician, are arguably the products of Cardenal the contemplative, who in contemplating God's work in the world and in society remains as enamoured of God as he was at the time of his departure for Gethsemani. His 'exteriorist' poetry, as he described it in the 1950s, became more and more cosmic, political and personal, linking his own contemplative life with his role as government minister.[50] Cardenal's hymn to the Nicaraguan fallen is a hymn to those who suffered and suffer today, many of them previously members of the community of Solentiname, and his words resound in a canticle of politics and metaphysics: 'When it's your turn to take the microphone, be on television, think of the ones who died . . . You represent them. They delegated you, the ones who died.'[51] Within that contemplation of the human there is the realization that the cosmic, matter and spirit, the living and the dead, are all part of that life of contemplation and politics, and the Cardenal of the 1990s, the post-politics Cardenal, returned to the canticles and the poetry of the contemplative of creation. The *Canto Cósmico* (*Cosmic Canticle*) extends to more than 500 pages, and in the words of Dinah Livingstone: 'the poet resumes and develops many of the themes that have fascinated him for decades: the science of matter and the cosmos; sky, stars and flying; the American Indians; plant and animal life rhythms; rhythm and harmony in the cosmos as a whole; love and attraction . . .'[52] In Cardenal's own words:

> The music of the spheres.
> A universe harmonious as a harp.
> Rhythm is repeated equal times.[53]

It is that music of change and revolution arising out of contemplation, the love of God and the Gospels, that shook Latin America and the Latin American Church at the time Cardenal was living in Solentiname. Other non-Latin Americans joined in service to God through the work of the churches in Latin America and they too suffered for trying to contemplate God in a harmonious universe. Like Cardenal, other American Catholics corresponded with and were influenced by Thomas Merton. One of those was the radical Jesuit Daniel Berrigan, who is the subject of the next chapter.

3

Daniel Berrigan SJ

The American Jesuit Daniel (Dan) Berrigan made an impact on the world of contemplation and politics because of his gift as writer and poet as well as his role of political activist, particularly within the non-violent movement against the Vietnam War, nuclear weapons and all aggressive actions by the USA against other countries and in other conflicts.[1] For those who resented his involvement in the political world he was a criminal, and indeed for a while he was among the FBI's ten most wanted people. For those who saw the connections between an honest response to the gospel values of peace, justice and solidarity he has been an inspiration. Together with Thomas Merton and Ernesto Cardenal he combined a religious aesthetic and a deep sense of prayer with an involvement in social issues and challenges to the status quo and to the uncritical Christian support for the aims and battles embraced by the state and by the military.

A contemplative Jesuit

Daniel Berrigan was born in Virginia, Minnesota, on 9 May 1921, the fifth of six boys born to Thomas and Frida Berrigan.[2] Later the family moved to Syracuse, New York, where Dan attended Catholic primary school – Jesuits were very much part of the history of Syracuse, having established the first mission in the area in 1656.[3] Both Dan and his close friend Jack St George were sure they wanted to become Catholic priests, and they requested brochures from several Catholic orders and congregations. Both applied to join the Jesuits in 1938 and travelled by train to Auriesville, New York, where they were interviewed. After receiving letters of acceptance they joined the Jesuits – at St Andrew-on-the-Hudson, the Jesuit novitiate near Poughkeepsie, New York – immediately after leaving secondary school in 1939.[4] Following Jesuit custom Berrigan made the thirty-day retreat (Ignatian Exercises) together with his classmates.[5] He later studied philosophy for two years at St Peter's in Jersey City, New Jersey (1946–9) and theology at Weston School of Theology in Cambridge, Massachusetts (1949–53). He was ordained as a priest on 21 June 1952 in the Weston chapel by Cardinal Richard Cushing. This was followed by a party at his parents' home.

In 1953 Berrigan travelled to France for his Jesuit tertian-ship (the period for every Jesuit between their novitiate and the religious profession in the Society of Jesus, during which they teach in a school or work in a parish), and came into con-tact with the French worker-priests. Already during the Jewish deportations from France some of them had volunteered to be deported in order to minister to their fellow captives. After the war economic conditions in France were difficult, and large numbers of Catholics joined the socialist and Communist parties, so that by the time Berrigan arrived in Paris priests in black cassocks were distrusted and numbers attending Mass had decreased. Attacks on the Catholic Church were custom-ary, accusing it of being servant to the establishment as it had been at the time of the French monarchy. Among those who led the worker-priests were the Jesuit Henri Perrin, who had ministered to Frenchmen sent to work at the German factories, and Abbé Pierre, a former Resistance leader who was challeng-ing the wealthier French to build affordable housing for the French working classes. The case of the worker-priests provided a strong challenge to the priestly ministry in the Americas because previously it was assumed that Christian communities or religious congregations would support the lives and works of Catholic priests financially so as to free them to minister full time and be available to administer the sacraments throughout the year. However, the phenomenon of worker-priests showed that there were certain individuals who wanted to move from a church-centred ministry to a way of life in which the priests were working as most people within society do, 'working in industry and living on their wages as workers'.[6]

Berrigan witnessed the controversy between Pope Pius XII and the worker-priests; Pius XII argued that their spirit was more dangerous than useful and ordered them to leave their factories and places of work and return to the traditional parishes. Some refused; nevertheless, the seeds of a new theology of the priesthood endorsed by the Second Vatican Council were already there and made an impact on the young Jesuit. During this time Berrigan also served at a US military base for 40 days, without feeling, as he would later, any challenges or problems of conscience at being surrounded by military personnel, their weapons and nuclear armaments already proliferating in post-war Europe. He only commented on the massive expenditure that such enterprise would need, and he did not like the fact that his senior chaplain wore uniform and carried a gun.

On his return to the USA Berrigan taught at Brooklyn Preparatory School, a Jesuit high school in Flatbush, until 1957, when he moved to Le Moyne College, Syracuse, New York, as associate professor of dogmatic theology. At the college he raised awareness about slums among the students, and some of them discovered that certain college benefactors were also slum landlords. The bishop was not pleased, and threatened to sack Berrigan, but his colleagues agreed that if Daniel were to be sacked they too would resign. As the bishop needed college lecturers, nothing happened in the end, and the students continued to help the hungry and the homeless.

In the meantime Berrigan's brother, Philip, had been ordained as a priest of the Josephites, a group of priests working with African Americans and very much part of those who supported racial equality in the USA.[7] Both brothers developed a challenging exchange, whereby some of Daniel's students were sent to work on the Congress of Racial Equality (CORE) in New Orleans, while bright but deprived African-American students attended Le Moyne College on scholarships. Daniel wanted to join Philip in a Freedom Ride march throughout the South but was denied permission. Instead, he visited Czechoslovakia, Hungary and South Africa. On his return he started speaking against the US involvement in Vietnam and became one of the co-founders of the Catholic Peace Fellowship.

Together with his brother Philip he became very active in the opposition to the Vietnam War and the drafting of young Americans in order to fight the Communist forces of North Vietnam. There is no doubt that Thomas Merton influenced some of his activities by discussing particular developments within the Vietnam campaign. For example, on 3 June 1965 Daniel Berrigan and two other activists, Jim Douglass and Bob McDole, visited Merton at Gethsemani in order to discuss the Second Vatican Council's Schema 13 ('The Church in the Modern World') and the alterations that were made in the article on war that discussed in particular the use of nuclear weapons by the USA.[8] In 1948 Berrigan had written to Thomas Merton praising *The Seven Storey Mountain*, but Merton never replied because his Abbot had forbidden him to reply to so many letters. By 1962 Berrigan and Merton were again exchanging regular correspondence, and one topic was the lack of freedom given Berrigan by his superiors for involvement in the civil rights movement of the South. Berrigan was ready to leave the Jesuits, and it was Merton who advised him against it, arguing that if he left, many of his followers would not continue striving for civil rights, justice and peace in American society. Due to these tensions Berrigan was sent to France on sabbatical during 1964, and when he returned he had changed from a well-behaved Jesuit into a self-assertive, conscientious objector to social injustice and violence of any kind – military, economic, social or racial.

A contemplative outlaw

In November 1964 Merton invited Berrigan and others for a three-day retreat at Gethsemani, with the theme 'Spiritual

Roots of Protest'. Those in attendance on 17 November were A. J. Muste, W. H. Ferry (Center for the Study of Democratic Institutions and the Fellowship of Reconciliation – FOR), Anthony Walsh of the Montreal Catholic Worker House, the Mennonite theologian John H. Yoder, John Oliver Nelson (previously national chair of FOR and professor at Yale Divinity School) and the Catholic activists Robert Cunnane, John Peter Grady, Tom Cornell, Jim Forest, Daniel and Philip Berrigan.[9] On Merton's suggestion there was to be no rigid agenda, and he gave a talk on 'The Monastic Protest: The Voice in the Wilderness'.[10] Daniel Berrigan celebrated Mass in English, a novelty at that time of customary Latin liturgies, and gave communion to Protestants present at the liturgy, a fact Merton deemed 'uncanonical' but 'simple and impressive'.[11]

Throughout the USA a whole generation of youth, mostly fresher ranks at colleges and universities, were questioning the rationality of war. They were reading Merton's essays, and many protestors and activists for peace corresponded with Merton and went on retreat to Merton's hermitage, because:

> Merton and his fellow retreatants believed that humanity was at a historic moment. A fundamental re-examination of existing values and radical actions were needed. Though Merton declined to participate in person in the revolutionary forces at work in the world, he continued to encourage Gandhian non-violent action.[12]

The escalation of hostilities against North Vietnam took place in August 1965 when, after confusing reports of an attack by Communist patrol boats on the US destroyer *Maddox* in the South China Sea's Gulf of Tonkin, President Johnson obtained a Congress resolution granting him all necessary measures to prevent further acts of aggression. US aircraft escalated the bombardment of North Vietnam. Most US voters still supported the war, despite the fact that by the end of 1965, 6,000 respected academics had appealed to the US government, in vain, to end it. The political climate in the USA was challenging – the civil rights movement was changing tactics from peaceful demonstrations to further actions after the shooting of Malcolm X in February 1965, and students staged a mass demonstration in Washington DC against the Vietnam War. In March 1965, the 82-year-old German-born Quaker Alice Herz set fire to herself in the streets of Detroit, emulating the actions of Vietnamese monks in order to protest against the bombardment of Vietnam; by the end of 1965 another protestor, Norman Morrison, who was holding his one-year-old daughter, burned himself in front of the Pentagon.[13] On 9 November 1965, Roger LaPorte, a Catholic volunteer at the Catholic Worker House of Hospitality on Chrystie Street in Manhattan, set himself on fire in front of the United Nations building. Berrigan and other non-violent activists had to regain a peaceful momentum, as public opinion was going against those who burned themselves. In the words of Merton:

> Certainly the sign was powerful because incontestable and final in itself (and how frightful!). It broke through the undifferentiated, uninterpretable noises, and it certainly must have hit many people awful hard. But in three days it becomes again contestable and in ten it is forgotten.[14]

Berrigan's words at LaPorte's funeral spoke of a sacrifice so that others could have life, and those words ignited Cardinal Spellman's pressure on the New York Jesuits to get rid of him.

As part of the staff of Jesuit Missions, Berrigan was forcefully sent to Latin America in order to report and write about the work of the Jesuits. In November 1965, he went to Cuernavaca (Mexico), on what was to be a four-month tour of the Jesuit missions, while student protests at Fordham University and many other forms of support showed that Berrigan had struck a chord among ordinary American Catholics. Berrigan's exile was even more controversial because it happened during the year the Second Vatican Council ended, proclaiming a new atmosphere of change and dialogue between the Church and the contemporary world. In the meantime, and coinciding with Christmas, Cardinal Spellman flew to Vietnam to minister to the US troops and to assure them that the Vietnam War was a war to keep Western civilization going. Finally, and after enormous pressure on the Jesuits, Berrigan returned to the USA on 8 March 1966, and on 11 March he spoke to a large crowd of reporters at New York's Biltmore Hotel, stating that he was back to oppose the Vietnam War and that his trip to Latin America had shown him that the resources used in Vietnam were needed to relieve poverty and suffering in Latin America.

He continued his affiliation with the peace movement by taking new duties as counsellor on religious matters at Cornell University, and in February 1968 had the opportunity to visit Vietnam. The North Vietnamese government had decided to honour the Buddhist Tet holiday by releasing three prisoners (three American fighter pilots), and asked for representatives of the US peace movement to collect them. Those chosen were Howard Zinn, historian and formerly World War Two army air force bombardier, and Daniel Berrigan. The three prisoners – Major Norris Overly, Captain John Black and Lieutenant J. G. David Methany – were delivered to the Hanoi hotel where Zinn and Berrigan were staying, and flew back to Laos with them. US Ambassador William Sullivan met them and insisted that the men were members of the US armed forces and therefore should return to the USA by military carrier; the original idea had been to give a boost to the peace movement by bringing them back in a commercial airliner accompanied by Zinn and Berrigan. However, Berrigan appreciated the opportunity to visit Indochina and to have sheltered from the bombs with so many defenceless children.

Contemplative cards

By March 1968, General William Westmoreland had requested 206,000 more troops, opinion polls showed that half the US population felt that their involvement in Vietnam was wrong, and the first trial of Philip Berrigan and others who had destroyed federal property had started.[15] They were freed on bail after the trial was over, pending a further appeal. Philip travelled to Cornell University to teach a course on non-violent resistance with Daniel, and planning started for another strong protest action that this time was to involve Daniel.

At 12.30 p.m. on 17 May 1968, nine protestors – seven men and two women, all Catholics – went to the Knights of Columbus Hall on 1010 Frederick Road, Catonsville, a suburb of Baltimore, stormed the offices and burned 378 files relating to the Selective Service Board. The raid took ten minutes, and the media, already alerted, filmed the burning operation, the singing and the praying of the Lord's Prayer that had as its two central participants Daniel and Philip Berrigan. Since 1965 the destruction of draft cards had carried a financial and possible penal penalty; nonetheless, after long conversations with his brother Daniel Berrigan recognized that there was no way out. The change had taken place: Daniel, who had challenged the ecclesiastical authorities with his discourse against Vietnam and against violence, had become a citizen who was challenging the state's legal right to draft young Americans to fight in another country against forces that had not directly attacked US citizens. Those 'enemy forces' were rather allied with political systems anathematized by the USA, and were fighting with the help of its enemies, such as China and the Soviet Union. In the words of Patrick O'Brien:

> The actions were, and are, essentially sacramental, visible signs of invisible lives. The burning of draft cards to make real the burning of children; the pouring of blood over weapons to reveal their real intent; the digging of graves on the White House lawn to symbolize the earth as a cemetery of our best hopes; the use of hammers on the cones of nuclear weapons to awaken us to the urgent need of the world for ploughshares to feed the hungry.[16]

Daniel and the Catonsville offenders stood trial on 7 October 1968. Philip and three others were re-offenders and were already in prison, having lost bail. However, Daniel Berrigan's involvement in violent protest and destruction of federal property amounted to a new phenomenon, as outlined by Polner and O'Grady: 'the Catholic Left and the secular antiwar movement had more or less converged, each with its own agenda but both with the identical aim of crippling the war effort.'[17] Hundreds of protestors were outside the court, and a full rally of the peace movement gathered. Inside, prompted by the judge, Daniel Berrigan spoke of his actions in terms of trying to prevent the burning of children and the spilling of the blood of the innocent on the American flag. At one point he asked the judge if they could all recite the Lord's Prayer, and so they did, all united in what Harvey Cox labelled 'a Pentecostal Moment'.[18] Still, the judge convicted them all: Daniel was given a three-year custodial sentence and left on bail pending an appeal; Philip was given three and a half years plus six years for his Baltimore raid. As always, their mother Frida Berrigan backed their cause.

Daniel returned to Cornell to rest, pray and write, troubled by the death of Thomas Merton and at the same time searching for further contemplation, for further visions of where God wanted him to go. His play on the Catonsville trial, *The Trial of the Catonsville Nine*, became one of the central literary events of his life and probably the most well-known of his writings, as the play was staged time after time by groups learning and discussing non-violence.[19] Cornell University restored Daniel to his job despite his conviction, and the support of many triggered in him the sense that he should delay his imprisonment by fleeing, as Philip had already done. The FBI searched churches and congregations for the two priests, and Daniel appeared and reappeared at peace rallies and meetings as a fugitive and FBI most wanted man between April and August 1970. On 11 August, he was arrested at his hiding place in Block Island, Rhode Island. His arrest coincided with the escalation of the war in Indochina, marked at the end of April 1970 by President Nixon's announcement that US forces had bombed and invaded Cambodia. In the meantime, Daniel served time at the medium-security Federal Correctional Institute in Danbury, Connecticut, together with Philip, who by then was in and out of different prisons for repeated destruction of federal property. While in prison, Daniel worked at the prison dental office, wrote liturgies, read and continued celebrating the Eucharist together with Philip.

However, there were also difficult moments. Daniel almost died of an allergic reaction while on a dental chair, and had to be rushed to an outside hospital to save his life. The incident triggered other illnesses, and Daniel became weak, with stomach problems and kidney ailments. In the summer of 1971 he became eligible for parole. When it was denied by the US Parole Board, he went on a hunger and work strike. His parole came through on 24 February 1972. As he left prison, a group was there to meet him and he returned to his apartment at Fordham University – to find it locked, and all his possessions in a corridor.

After that initial disappointment he found himself invited to deliver hundreds of lectures, give university courses and address rallies. Despite his arthritis he became a lecturer, spending lots of time with students and joining local groups in their own protests. He became poet in residence at Fordham University and has continued a life of contemplation, prayer, writing and support for others, despite the fact that his younger years were filled with political activism and a sense of inner conversion following his understanding of the gospel under difficult material and emotional conditions.

A contemplative writer

It would be possible to argue that Daniel Berrigan has been an active campaigner for peace and not a contemplative. However, his many writings, including several collections of poems and biblical commentaries, suggest a total complementarity between active protest and contemplative consciousness that becomes the foundation for any social or political activity.[20] For example, struck by the 9/11 attacks on New York and Washington, DC, he wrote not out of his own active commitment to peace or his own activities of that day, but out of a personal, prayerful reflection on what had happened in New York, a lament for a common suffering humanity.[21] What came out was a very personal commentary on the book of Lamentations, and he had the courage to give his manuscript, critical of US policy, to Colleen Kelly, who had lost her brother on 9/11 – Kelly's brother, Bill, was at the World Trade Center that morning, attending a breakfast conference at the Windows on the World restaurant. At 9.23 a.m. he sent his last message, saying that he was trapped on the 106th floor. Thus, Kelly's initial reaction to Berrigan's writing was of disagreement, as she wrote in the Foreword to his book:

> Were it not for Dan's beautiful poetic verse, I'm not sure I could have finished the book you now hold. It is painful to read. I suppose that most will find this so, not just those of us who lost someone they love so fiercely on September 11th. Why does it hurt? Its raw indictment of our culture's role in the violence is laid bare. My first impulse is to disagree, to take offence.[22]

However, Kelly's further reaction was one of recognition that to lament is a universal phenomenon and that the universality of the phenomenon leads to questions of faith, the contemplation of the grieving subject in order to ask further questions about those responsible for those grieving moments, too common in our contemporary world. Thus, she concluded, 'We must look into the pit of Ground Zeros all over – New York, Kabul, Zion – and let our tears flow.'[23]

This is one of the reasons why Daniel Berrigan's contemplative writings go so deep into the consciousness of those who are attuned to an honest search for authenticity in their Christian life: his beautiful poetic verse speaks plainly of human creation and involvement in violence and the need to reject such violence. In rejecting terrorist violence, for example, Berrigan speaks the truth when he compares the grief and mercy of Lamentations with the events of 9/11. He reads the Scriptures, asking God for guidance, and the message comes clear: 'Because we had sinned, the poet insisted, because long since we had fallen to idolatries, to worship of money and weaponry and domination and betrayal.'[24]

This contemplative stance with the Scriptures beside him has been consistent for the past 30 years, in that after his prison experience Berrigan developed a very strong sense of the universality of the phenomenon of empire, through the metaphors of the beast and the reading of writings from the Bible that came out of periods of persecution, annihilation and prison. For some of Paul's letters come out of his experience of prison, and the writings related to Lamentations and the book of Daniel, to cite just a few, arise from the experience of a people who, feeling vulnerable, rediscover the fact that their oppressive situation is derived from their forgetfulness and their own forgetting of God as the only supreme authority. The message of Daniel, for example, provides a contemporary agenda and a prophetic challenge because, in Berrigan's words, 'there are the principalities of today to be confronted, their idols and thrice-stoked furnaces and caves of lions, their absurd self-serving images and rhetoric'.[25] For it is that challenging contemplation of God's values vis-à-vis the world that makes Berrigan an uncomfortable contemplative for others around him, because he does not compromise his choice of Christianity and his reading of the Scriptures. In his choice of texts for a book portraying icons – including an icon in which Rutilio Grande, the Jesuit assassinated in El Salvador in 1977, is holding the Holy Child of El Salvador – he wrote: 'The Child, surrogate and symbol of martyred Salvador. "Now" (say the eyes of Jesus, the burning eyes of Rutilio), "is the point clear?" '[26]

Towards contemplation and politics

In January 1973, less than a year after his release from prison, Daniel Berrigan took part in a four-day gathering held in Huddersfield, sponsored by the Student Christian Movement of the UK. At that meeting the radical activists with Christian roots looked at their own understanding of spirituality, and the prophetic words of Alistair Kee prepared the ground for a forthcoming Pentecostal experience of prophetic activism when he argued that 'unlike the politicos who have no time for religion, unlike the religious who have no time for the political, the new situation requires a personal integration of two traditions'.[27] Within that same gathering Berrigan spoke of his experience and the American experience of confronting the beast – that is, the American empire in its violent state forms – and compared the experience of being in jail 'to an early monastic experience'.[28] That contemplative capability in Berrigan's life to deal with God in the contemporary world by 'a personal integration of two traditions' is something that comes more naturally to Roman Catholics, particularly Jesuits, than to Protestants. However, what comes very naturally to all, and unites common humanity, is the search for God's will and for God's presence in the world: the contemplative and the political united and dependent on each other; change is allowed through a spiritual life that challenges the possibility of equating all the actions of the state with the Kingdom of God and a single manifestation of God's presence with the whole reality of the Kingdom.

It is clear that a deep sense of contemplation through the Scriptures and the Eucharist led Daniel Berrigan to continual responses to traumatic situations of war and non-violence within the context of the USA and its involvement in Vietnam. Merton, Cardenal and Berrigan reflected in an American context on the possibilities of contemplation and politics in Latin America. It is there where the majority of Christians of the world reside and it is there where Dr Sheila Cassidy, the subject of the next chapter, found her own taste of contemplation and politics within the context of Chile under the Pinochet regime.

4

Sheila Cassidy

At the end of December 1975, a young British doctor, Sheila Cassidy, left Santiago Airport covered with a poncho, and on landing at Heathrow Airport in London became one of the greatest stories in the history of the medical profession and the Catholic Church. Dr Cassidy had been arrested and tortured for operating on a wounded guerrilla fighter, having been called by Catholic priests and nuns who, in defiance of the law, were protecting two guerrilla fighters and their loved ones from arrest and probably murder by Pinochet's security services.

Sheila Cassidy, in one single act, caught the imagination of those who promise to cure and heal human beings when they qualify as medical doctors, and she also caught the imagination of those who, due to their Christian beliefs and Christian lives, had gone to live and work with the poor and the marginalized of Latin America at the time of the military regimes. In the words of Michael Hollings, 'Sheila's reaction to a situation of human need blew up, created a situation and hit many people in the world.'[1]

This chapter deals with Sheila Cassidy's ordeal in Chile, not in order to state the same facts that she narrated so vividly in her two autobiographical accounts but to search for the signs of a restless contemplative who has longed for God all her life and who was involved in the medical struggles of the poor in Chile, where she met other Christians who were also searching for God through prayer and lives of service.[2] In Cassidy's own words,

He or she has led me a merry dance into the torture chamber and out, into the convent and out, and then through 20 years of the most satisfying work a woman could wish for. Now I have emerged into a sunlit meadow and I feel God's love like the sun on my back. I have no idea what joy or suffering the future may bring but I am ready for either.[3]

After her Chilean experience, she continued serving the terminally ill in England, and throughout her retirement she has continued working in counselling others through her own medical practice of Cognitive Analytical Therapy (CAT).

Contemplative beginnings

Sheila Cassidy decided to become a doctor when she was 15, and at 17 gained university entrance. By then she was living in Australia, to which her family had emigrated in 1949.[4] However, her marks didn't garner a university scholarship and she spent another year preparing to repeat her entry exams, entering medical school in March 1956.[5] She was also aware of a possible calling to become a nun. In 1958, she transferred from the University of Sydney to the University of Oxford, and qualified as a doctor in 1963. During two years of residency in Oxford she decided to specialize in plastic surgery, and met Consuelo, a Chilean doctor with a scholarship to Oxford. Two and a half years later they met once again, in Leicester, and shared a flat. It was through Consuelo and her friends that Sheila Cassidy started learning about Chile, and she became fascinated by the country and the social processes unfolding with the election of a socialist, Salvador Allende, as its president in 1970. Thus, on 4 December 1971 Cassidy and her chow dog, Winston, departed by boat to Chile in order to join Consuelo and take a break from the pressures imposed by the National Health Service on junior doctors (while in Chile she decided to do the internships and exams necessary to become qualified as a doctor there).

She witnessed the military coup that took place on 11 September 1973. However, she returned to England in August

1974 in order to see her ailing father, who died that December. In January 1975, she returned to Chile and started work at the Posta 4, one of the quietest national health hospitals in Santiago, later moving to the Posta 3 in Chacabuco, another quiet hospital that cared for shanty-town dwellers. However, given the shortage of medical facilities the Catholic Church had managed to staff some small facilities for the poor, and Sheila Cassidy started helping in the new clinic in the Población El Salto. There she started learning first hand of the work by the Catholic Church on behalf of the politically persecuted, the unemployed and those disfavoured by the military government because of their previous support for the socialist government of Salvador Allende.

Contemplation and torture

Sheila Cassidy's arrest and torture coincided with a very difficult time for the Catholic Church in Chile that culminated with the incident at Malloco near Santiago, in October 1975, when priests and nuns decided to shelter armed subversives wanted by Pinochet's security forces.[6] On 15 October, agents of the *Dirección de Inteligencia Nacional* (DINA) discovered that the high command of the *Movimiento de Izquierda Revolucionario* (MIR), the only armed group opposing the military, was living on a farm in Malloco. Those living there included Andrés Pascal Allende, leader of the MIR, and Nelson Gutiérrez. Since the death of Miguel Henríquez, leader of the MIR, Andrés Pascal, nephew of President Allende, had taken over the leadership of all military operations conducted by the MIR. The DINA had managed to arrest, torture and make disappear hundreds of members of the MIR, but they had not found Pascal Allende.[7]

As the DINA agents opened fire on the property, two members of the MIR protected their leaders who, together with their partners and a baby, escaped through the fields. While the baby was left in the custody of a local person the five fugitives reached the main road, where they intercepted a car and escaped into the city. The fugitives sought refuge with Catholic priests, and were given refuge in secret locations within ecclesiastical properties. On the morning of 16 October 1975, Fr Cristián Precht informed Cardinal Silva Henríquez, and they deliberated what to do.[8] To the Cardinal it was clear that if the fugitives were handed over to the DINA they would be tortured and killed; therefore they had to be protected and handed over to foreign embassies instead. In his memoirs, he is clear that while others thought the Church was being used by terrorists, he saw instead human beings cornered by the security forces, who if discovered would be killed without due legal process. The Cardinal used the parable of the Good Samaritan in order to justify his actions and those of the Catholic Church.[9]

Bishop Alvear coordinated the protection of the five fugitives, and Frs Gerardo Whelan, Rafael Maroto, Fermín Donoso and Patricio Cariola moved them to different parishes, convents and religious houses. In the case of Nelson Gutiérrez, who had a bullet wound in his leg, the priests asked a British doctor – Sheila Cassidy – to operate and administer antibiotics. Fr Cariola convinced the fugitives to give up their arms, and Fr Fernando Salas dispersed them in different places throughout Santiago. However, on 2 November the DINA located the fifth fugitive at the house of Fr Whelan, and arrested them both. Immediately the DINA proceeded to arrest all foreign clergy involved, and attacked the Columban Fathers' house in Santiago, where Sheila Cassidy was staying. On 4 November Cardinal Silva Henríquez and Bishop Valech met with the Minister of the Interior, General César Raúl Benavides, in order to discuss the tense and difficult situation.

In the meantime, Fr Cariola managed to bring Nelson Gutiérrez to the Vatican Embassy and Andrés Pascal Allende to the Embassy of Costa Rica. However, the tribunals wanted to interview Frs Cariola and Salas, and they remained as guests of the Cardinal in his house. Days later, Silva Henríquez met with General Pinochet in order to discuss the situation, and the general arrest of foreign clergy that was taking place all over Chile. Pinochet requested that Pro Paz, the church-run office that protected those persecuted by the military regime, be closed down, and the Cardinal in turn asked Pinochet for the request to be put in writing. However, the Cardinal assured him that the humanitarian defence of the persecuted by the Church could not end and that if an organization such as Pro Paz were not allowed legally to exist he would hide fugitives under his bed if necessary. Pinochet requested the closure of Pro Paz on 11 November, and while the Cardinal agreed, he wrote a letter stating his Christian position towards human-rights abuses and the conviction that the Church in Chile under his leadership could not cease to help those in need.

During November 1975, hundreds of foreign missionaries were expelled from Chile, and the DINA continued its own dismantling of the MIR and the Communist Party. Frs Cariola and Salas turned themselves in to the courts and were brought to the Capuchinos annexe of Santiago Prison. As they entered the prison, under heavy escort and handcuffed, the prisoners lined up outside their cells and long applause followed. When the Cardinal heard the story in Rome, where he had gone to request the Pope's advice, he felt proud, and wrote: 'they were my priests, the priests of my Church, the priests of the Church in Chile, that was their blessed madness'.[10] While in Rome, Paul VI supported him and publicly spoke of Frs Cariola and Salas as 'martyrs of Christian charity', while assuring the Cardinal that he had all his support for the defence of human life in Chile. In December, Silva Henríquez officially closed Pro Paz, and the last of the DINA's prisoners, the lawyer José Zalaquett, was able to leave Chile and go into exile.

Throughout this crisis the DINA had Sheila Cassidy in their hands. She had not been aware of the importance of the battle of Malloco, and as she had no contact with Chilean revolutionaries she took the newspaper headlines as evidence of 'yet another confrontation between the military and some resistance workers and, knowing the lack of freedom of the press, wondered how much of it was true'.[11] However, the event became reality on Tuesday 21 October, when Fr Fernando Salas, one of her friends, asked her if she would be prepared to treat a man with a bullet wound to his leg, a request that had been approved by Bishop Enrique Alvear.[12] Her answer was positive and she later wrote: 'I did not weigh up the pros and cons: a doctor faced with a wounded man does not weigh as on a balance the worth of that man against the worth of other possible patients.'[13] The priest commented that the wounded man had been involved in the shooting at Malloco and that she should go to an office in Santiago city centre, from where somebody else would take her to his location. At that office she met her contact, an American Sister of Notre Dame, Helen Nelson, who took her to her own convent, where they were greeted by Andrés Pascal Allende's girlfriend, Mary Ann Beausire. Here Cassidy examined Nelson Gutiérrez, the hidden wounded man, finding three bullet wounds, the entry and exit of one bullet, and the entry wound of another that she could not feel using her instruments. She decided that it would be better to treat the wound with antibiotics and dressings rather than searching for the bullet, and left prescription notes and promised to check on him 48 hours later. On 23 October she returned to the convent and met Nelson Gutiérrez's partner, Mariela, who told her that Gutiérrez was feverish and that they had tried to move him to a safer place but that he could not stand. Having examined him, Sheila Cassidy became worried for Gutiérrez's health, and advised him to seek asylum in a foreign embassy that would provide safe passage and adequate medical treatment. Gutiérrez and Mariela agreed (although as Mariela had left her baby with a neighbour when they escaped from DINA agents, she was naturally reluctant to leave Chile without him), but Mary Ann Beausire declined. It is important to remember that members of the MIR had orders from their high command not to seek asylum, and even those who survived torture and reappeared abroad alive were distrusted by their comrades.

Sheila went home and thought that was the end of her active role as Good Samaritan. However, on the following day she had to attend another meeting, where she was informed that the Vatican Ambassador had agreed to grant asylum to Nelson and

Mariela but that any medical treatment would have to be given within the Vatican Embassy as it was too dangerous to negotiate the possibility of treating him at a hospital. Sheila Cassidy would have to go with them; this time she was reluctant but finally agreed.[14] After a full night shift at the Posta (local hospital), she headed for the Vatican Embassy, disguised as a foreign nun under the name of Sister Elizabeth and carrying the surgical tools and medications necessary to perform surgery on Nelson Gutiérrez's leg. On entering the Embassy, she found to her relief that another doctor was already there, and she left and went home.

A week later she was still working her shifts at the hospital. But as a friend of hers who was a nun had a bad cold, Cassidy asked Fr William Halliden, head of the Columbans, if she could stay at their main house in Larraín Gandarillas Street. Enriqueta, the maid, took good care of her, and in between hospital shifts Cassidy visited her friend. On 1 November, the Feast of All Saints, she went to the nearby Italian Parish for evening Mass and only returned around 9 p.m. to her home, where supper was announced for 10 p.m. She decided to visit her ill friend, and as they started to pray together they heard a scream. Cassidy and Fr Halliden rushed downstairs and saw Enriqueta lying on the floor in a large pool of blood. As they reached her the firing started, the bullets destroying windows and walls. Ten minutes later a group of men knocked the door down and entered. Fr Halliden thought they were coming to help them but instead the intruders were happy to know they had found Sheila Cassidy, the doctor who had helped Nelson Gutiérrez.[15] They took her in a car towards the hills of Santiago and after they entered a large villa with an iron door, Sheila Cassidy realized that they had arrived at the Villa Grimaldi, one of the DINA's most notorious torture centres and at that time headquarters of the Metropolitan Brigade of the DINA, to which so many members of the MIR had been taken, never to be heard of again.[16] Cassidy was interrogated under torture. In her own words: 'What happened to me is typical of what happens to political prisoners in countries where torture has become institutionalized as an instrument of interrogation and repression.'[17]

She was tied to a metallic bed and given electric shocks in between questioning. She had learnt in medical school that 'pain had three components: the actual pain experienced, the memory of past pain and the future of past pain'.[18] Thus, at the start of the torture sessions she was stronger because her body had no memory of the pain and agony she was in. However, as hours passed she became more vulnerable to pain and memory. She tried to respond to the questions by misleading her interrogators, who wanted to know who had asked her to treat Gutiérrez, and she gave a false name and a false location. A man playing the role of 'kind' interrogator ordered her release and talked to her, but after a short interval the interrogators pushed her into a car and went searching for the house she had mentioned, which of course didn't exist. But they did find a colonial-style white house that had the characteristics of one described by Cassidy during interrogation and that was located in Obispo Subercaseaux Avenue. They stopped near the house and a large security operation started, with agents running and vehicles gathering while Cassidy remained in the back of a police van. The security services were excited at the prospect of finding the hiding place of Andrés Pascal Allende and Nelson Gutiérrez, but as they entered the house they realized that it was empty and was being painted. They took Cassidy back to the Villa Grimaldi.

The torture with electricity went on for a few hours more, and Sheila Cassidy finally led her torturers to the house where she had treated Nelson Gutiérrez. Her confession led to the arrest of an American priest and of Martín Hernández, a member of the MIR, but didn't lead them to Andrés Pascal Allende. On the following morning the British Ambassador asked the Chilean authorities for her protection, but the night was long and the DINA agents continued their interrogation. They were incensed to hear that Nelson Gutiérrez was at the Vatican Embassy, but the senior ranking officials present were very clear that no attack on the Embassy was to take place. There were so many church personnel involved that the DINA agents didn't know whether to start arresting large numbers of American missionaries, including a number of nuns. Because the DINA wanted to know the whereabouts of Andrés Pascal Allende, Sheila Cassidy underwent a third session of torture. They showed her photographs of priests and made her listen to taped conversations, in an effort to identify the foreign priests involved in moving around the wanted members of the MIR.

She was kept tied to the metallic bed after that interrogation but not given electric shocks, most probably because the agents had gone looking for the priests involved. It was during that lonely moment at Villa Grimaldi that Sheila Cassidy prayed and contemplated Jesus' passion on the cross. In her words:

> Most of all I remember a curious feeling of sharing in Christ's passion. Sick and numb with pain and fear, and spreadeagled so vulnerably on the bunk, it came to me that this was perhaps a little how it had been for him one Friday so many years before.[19]

In the early morning she was taken to another room where there were other prisoners. There she rested on a bed and was cared for by Francisca, a young Chilean socialist. Throughout the day she was taken to an office for several rounds of questioning, and hours later was made to write a confession that was dictated to her. During that day Cassidy heard a man being tortured and saw him being dragged along by the interrogators; she assumed that the man was Martín Hernández.

A few days later Sheila Cassidy was transferred to Tres Alamos, a camp in Santiago where nearly 600 prisoners were kept. However, she was located within Cuatro Alamos, a detention facility within Tres Alamos managed by the DINA. A man calling himself a doctor tried to hypnotize her, and she felt that the food was worse than at the Villa Grimaldi, where food at least came from the same kitchen set up for the guards. The 'doctor' brought her parts of a Bible and some reading material, and she decided, after a good night's sleep, to pray:

> After breakfast I sat on my bunk and gave myself seriously to thinking. God was very real to me, and I asked myself and Him just what it was He had in mind. There was no blinding light or voice from behind the mountains (in my experience there never is!) but it seemed to me that if I was going to spend all day alone I must spend a great deal of it in prayer.[20]

On Friday of that week the British Consul, Derek Fernyhough, finally came to visit her, and all the anxieties and fears she had borne for days burst forth in tears. The prison commander was present and they were forced to conduct the conversation in Spanish. The British Consul assured her that the British government was seeking a diplomatic solution to her imprisonment, and brought perfume, soap and cigarettes, as well as a long list of those who had sent messages of support and greetings. He asked her if she had been well treated and she replied 'Yes'; however, as the commander was shouting over a phone call she conveyed the following words to the British Consul: 'Mains, Derek, mains'. He didn't understand, but cabled the words to London, where it became clear that Sheila Cassidy had been tortured with electricity.[21]

On 10 November 1975 she was taken under guard to the office of the Military Prosecutor, who asked further questions and was interested in knowing whether she had shot a member of the DINA from the house in Larraín Gandarillas Street. At the end of the interview, which was to continue the following day, the Prosecutor suggested to her that she would be tried according to Chilean law. On return to her cell Cassidy became afraid that the death penalty would be applied, and as usual talked to God:

> Bewildered and afraid, I faced God. I had been so sure of his plans for me: I was to return to England and become a nun, to dedicate my life totally to his service. Had he changed his mind? Or perhaps I had read the signs wrong. That my life was to be one of service to him I knew beyond any doubt, but it had never

occurred to me that the service might be undertaken some-where very different from where I had chosen.[22]

On the following day Sheila Cassidy was brought to the military courts, where throughout the day her statement was taken and typed. With her there was a worker-priest who had been arrested for aiding members of the MIR and who, after the ordeal was over, returned to his shanty town to continue earning his keep and living the gospel in poverty. The Prosecutor told her finally that she was under the jurisdiction of the military courts and that she would be moved to the *Casa Correccional*, a common detention centre for women and outside the jurisdiction of the DINA. After signing a statement to the effect that she had not been tortured by the DINA she was moved to the *Correccional*, where to her surprise a group of nuns in white habits hugged her and kissed her, rejoicing that finally she had appeared among them. She was able to take a shower, the first one since her arrest, and talked to other prisoners and Sister Augusta, who explained that those at the *Correccional* were prisoners who had not been charged. The Good Shepherd Sisters ran the establishment in order to rehabilitate young delinquents, so that the atmosphere was better than in other detention centres. She had some supper, and as the military courts had imposed solitary confinement, was once again locked up on her own.

On 13 November 1975, Cassidy was allowed outside her cell and ate some stew brought by other prisoners. However, she missed the Eucharist and requested to see the prison chaplain, Fr Patricio Gajardo, not realizing that a week earlier he had been arrested, together with two lay workers of the Committee for Peace. They were interrogated at the Villa Grimaldi, and one of the women among them was raped. All of them left the country on their release. On 14 November Cassidy was once again brought in front of the military courts. There she saw four priests who had been involved in the sheltering of the persecuted members of the MIR: the priest she had met at Tres Alamos, as well as Fathers Fernando Salas,

Patricio Cariola and Gerard Whelan. The British Consul was also there, and Cassidy was able to tell him all that had happened, while both agreed that they would follow the court's proceedings, hoping for a possible release. However, the British Embassy informed the Foreign Office in London of her torture and ill-treatment by the DINA. Later, a Jesuit from the San Ignacio School arrived and went to buy sandwiches and fruit for all the prisoners and their guards. Cassidy commented:

> Never will I forget that meal: in the gloomy windowless hall outside the Fiscal's office we shared our lunch with the embarrassed wardens. We sat there laughing and talking like a group of children at a picnic: three Chilean Jesuits, an American missionary priest, a Chilean worker-priest and an English woman doctor, none of us knowing if we were going to be freed or given a long prison sentence.[23]

The military judge decided to free her. She called the British Consul, requesting to stay at his home, but was advised to go to the British Embassy as soon as her release papers were signed at the *Casa Correccional* because of the danger that the DINA might kidnap her again, being displeased at the outcome of the military court's proceedings. Hernán Montealegre, a human-rights lawyer, offered to accompany her to the *Correccional* and to stay there until the British Consul arrived. Montealegre drove her and the guards back to the *Correccional*, where it was made clear to her that as she had been arrested under the state of siege legislation it was not possible to release her without permission from the National Office of Detainees (SENDET). She returned to her quarters with other prisoners and decided to wait until Monday, when the administrative offices would be re-opened.

Contemplation and death

However, the following day, a Saturday, a senior nun came to tell her to collect her belongings as she was being transferred to Tres Alamos once again. She refused to move and the British Consul and her lawyers were called. Finally, all agreed that co-operation was appropriate, and Sheila Cassidy was driven by the British Consul to Tres Alamos. Her surprise was enormous when, after routine procedures at the main office, she was handed over across the gate to a civilian member of the DINA and once again kept in a cell at the DINA detention centre of Cuatro Alamos.

Cassidy had some personal effects that were brought by the American nuns via the British Consul, and she quickly established a daily routine, not knowing what was going to happen to her in the future. Within that routine she decided to read the Old Testament and to study the Bible in the afternoons, as well as spend time in prayer. In her own words:

> It was curiously difficult, perhaps because I was so unsettled and frightened, but I had learnt long ago that prayer depends on the will and not on the emotions. So I gave my time and my anguish to God and tried to understand what it was he wanted of me.[24]

The British Consul visited her once again and she was joined by two companions in her cell: Javiera, a young prisoner she had met at the Villa Grimaldi, and Isabel, a middle-aged woman who had been arrested a few days earlier. On 24 November Sheila Cassidy was once again transferred, together with two other woman, to the *Casa Correccional*. She was led to a wooden barrack where she was warmly greeted by several women prisoners, including some she had met before. She was given some salad, and a new experience of common life and material sharing started for her. There were 120 women in the camp, mostly in their twenties, and more people than beds, so that some had to take turns sleeping on the floor. There was no hot water, and rations from a central kitchen were insufficient to keep people healthy, particularly those who were pregnant, ill or had recently been tortured at the Villa Grimaldi. Therefore, although some families could afford to bring extra food for their relatives, the rule developed by the prisoners was to pool food and give priority to those who needed extra nourishment.

Once again Sheila Cassidy thought she was going to be in the camp only a few days, but the feeling among some prisoners was that it was probably going to be a few months, as most of the prisoners stayed there for a year or more until their cases were either heard by the military courts, they were expelled from the country or taken in as refugees by a foreign country. Twice a week there were visits, and apart from the British Consul she received visits from the American nuns, who had become her close friends. Maybe the most striking aspect of the visit was the reunion of infants with their mothers who were prisoners, and Cassidy 'realized once again that their suffering had a dimension that I would never share nor even begin to comprehend'.[25] Some of them could only come to see their mothers every few months as their families lived far from Santiago; some didn't have the means to visit more often.

As Cassidy, like all the prisoners, was denied the possibility of a priest celebrating the Eucharist, some American sisters brought her a consecrated host, from which she consumed a small piece every morning. She found time to pray without being disturbed by other prisoners and was also asked by a small group of Christians – among a majority of Marxist prisoners – to lead a Sunday prayer service. Some of those who were not Christians also came, and there was a group of around 50 prisoners who heard a passage of the Bible and prayed for the needs of prisoners, their families and others in general. Thus, in her assessment 'robbed of my house, my possessions, my friends, my work and my freedom to come and go as I pleased, I knew an unbelievable freedom of spirit'.[26]

Out of her prisoner's experience, Sheila Cassidy learned that most of those young women were in prison, and had endured torture and humiliation, because of their beliefs in a political system, in a new society, in a just world. They were disciplined revolutionaries who had learnt how to confront adversity, discomfort and death little by little, by daily denials of the self, by refusing to stay in bed, by eating and drinking no more than necessary, by sharing their time and their efforts with those who needed them. The ideology of socialism was close to that of a Christian communal life, and the community reflections and ideological conscientization of these women similar to those of Christian reflection groups. Thus, the lessons of service given by non-Christians impressed the contemplative and prayerful Sheila Cassidy, in such a way that towards the end of her first autobiography, and commenting on the communal spirit of self-denial that permeated the lives of the women prisoners around her, she wrote:

> The final victory over their terror of pain and physical death is the last of a thousand victories and defeats in the war which is fought daily and hourly in the human mind and soul: the war in the overcoming of self. Dissected and examined in detail this is a most unglamorous battle and to the outsider seems absurd; but it is the constant denying of the natural human urge to stay in bed longer than necessary, to eat or drink more than is justifiable, to be intolerant of the stupid, and to accumulate more than a fair share of this world's goods, that makes possible the gradual freeing of the human spirit.[27]

On 23 December 1975, Sheila Cassidy heard on the radio that no further charges would be filed against her; at the same time the military government's amnesty for Christmas included 30 women who were at the camp, so that they had reason to rejoice. They all prepared to celebrate Christmas, and the camp commander allowed the prison chaplain to say Mass for the prisoners; Cassidy was ordered to prepare things and gather the prisoners. A feast followed, in which a Harrods cake brought by the British Ambassador was shared, and in the evening the women prisoners sang as loud as they could for the men prisoners across the compound, particularly those in solitary confinement – comrades, husbands, boyfriends – until the order came to be silent and Christmas was over. Then, the voices of the male prisoners were heard and tears rolled down the cheeks of Sheila Cassidy and many other prisoners.

On 26 December the British Consul and his wife Grace came to visit Cassidy, bringing some cold turkey and ham – and the news that most probably she would be released the following Monday. Over the weekend the radio bulletin announced that she was to leave Chile on the British Caledonian flight of 29 December. On that day, all prisoners were told to move to the visitors' building, and Sheila Cassidy was taken to another building to sign papers. She was then driven to the airport, where the British Ambassador and Consul were waiting with an air ticket and a temporary passport. As she boarded the bus that brought passengers to the plane, she waved to a sea of people who had gathered to say goodbye to her. A moving tribute to her service to the poor was written by Bishop Jorge Hourton after her departure.[28]

Contemplation in political action

After her return to the UK, and 18 months (1976–7) of political activism on behalf of prisoners and exiles from Chile, Sheila Cassidy spent some time at the Benedictine abbey at Ampleforth pursuing her possible vocation as a religious-contemplative. However, she came to realize that her vocation was, after all, in medicine.[29] She worked for many years as a medical director of a hospice for cancer patients in Plymouth, and has remained there as part-time doctor and psychotherapist.[30]

The lessons of her life are not different from those offered by Merton, Berrigan or Cardenal: contemplation and prayer lead Christians into a commitment to the poor and the marginalized that has enormous consequences for one's life. Further, it is through periods of daily prayer and contemplation of God that life becomes self-giving and a challenge to those of society's structures and political decisions that do not allow for the poor and the marginalized to be central to politicians' decisions. If Sheila Cassidy's following of 'Love Thy Neighbour' permeated all her life as a doctor, the 'love of God and neighbour' challenged her to the extreme through imprisonment, torture and exile. The next chapter explores the life of Archbishop Desmond Tutu, who throughout a sustained period of South African history challenged the political authorities with a Christian message of equality that came out of his own daily contemplation of 'the God of the rainbow'.

5

Archbishop Desmond Tutu

For many years, we were accustomed to watching images on our televisions of unrest and violence in South Africa. Some of us attended vigils in Trafalgar Square in front of the South Africa High Commission. In recalling those images of the 1980s, Archbishop Desmond Tutu stands out as one of those who seems always to have been present on our screens, always happy, always dancing, but directly opposed to any racial discrimination and to the system of apartheid. When, in 1984, Tutu was awarded the Nobel Prize for Peace it was globally recognized that a man of prayer and deep contemplation was making a central contribution not only to the unity of humanity but to a further understanding of God and his work within the contemporary world and for a future just society. Always direct in his assessment of contemporary issues, in his Nobel Lecture Tutu told the distinguished audience the following story:

> Once a Zambian and a South African, it is said, were talking. The Zambian then boasted about their Minister of Naval Affairs. The South African asked: 'But you have no navy, no access to the sea. How then can you have a Minister of Naval Affairs?' The Zambian retorted, 'Well, in South Africa you have a Minister of Justice, don't you?'[1]

Born to contemplate

Desmond Tutu was born in 1931 in Klerkdorp, Transvaal. His father was a teacher and he studied at Johannesburg Bantu High School, a school popularly known as Madibane High after its charismatic principal.[2] The Native Lands Act of 1913, by which Black Africans could not buy or lease other lands, caused great suffering for traditional Black areas. Black Africans had to carry passes to go into White areas, and urban settlements did not have enough employment possibilities for those who lived within them. Thus, Tutu's upbringing took place amid the regular arrest of Africans who trespassed into other areas, failed to carry 'pass books' and so on. It is estimated that 'an average of 250,000 people a year were arrested for violations of the pass laws between 1916 and 1981'.[3] After leaving school Tutu trained as a teacher at Pretoria Bantu Normal College, and in 1954 graduated from the University of South Africa. This was the year the South African government decided to take African education out of the hands of the churches and proclaimed that Africans were destined for certain kinds of labour and that full education was a path for Europeans and not for Africans.[4] Within that difficult educational climate Tutu worked as a teacher for three years and started his studies for the Anglican priesthood, being ordained as a deacon in 1960 and as a priest in 1961, the year in which South Africa withdrew from the Commonwealth due to protests within that organization against the South African regime led by the African states, Canada and India. Between 1962 and 1966 he studied in London, where he completed his Bachelor of Divinity degree and Master's degree in theology. On his return to South Africa he joined the staff of the Federal Theological Seminary and was a chaplain at the University of Fort Hare, returning to England as Associate Director of the Theological Educational Fund of the World Council of Churches, based in Kent. In 1975, Tutu was appointed Dean of St Mary's Cathedral in Johannesburg, the first Black African to hold a major post in South Africa's metropolitan area. In 1976 came his appointment as Bishop of Lesotho and in 1978 as General Secretary of the South African Council of Churches, the representative organization of the World Council of Churches in South Africa.[5] From 1985 to 1986 he was Bishop of Johannesburg, and from 1986 until his retirement Archbishop of Cape Town.

Tutu's first public dialogue with the state took place in 1976, and can be considered the coming out of the contemplative supporter of social justice and of the Kingdom of God. When Tutu became Dean of St Mary's Cathedral, he didn't seek permission to live in a White-only area, but decided to live in the South Western Townships or Soweto. On 6 May 1976 Tutu wrote a letter to John Vorster, Prime Minister of South Africa, resident of Cape Town, outlining the possibilities of bloodshed in the country.[6] That was his second letter to Vorster; the first one dated back to 1972, when Tutu had been refused a South African passport, which he needed to take up his post as Associate Director of the Theological Educational Fund. After Vorster's intercession, Tutu was given a passport. In a personal letter that later became public, Tutu wrote of his fears for violence in a country that recently had supported a national rugby team against Argentina and that made all South Africans, White and Black, a people united through sport:

> I am writing to you, Sir, because I have a growing nightmarish fear that unless something drastic is done very soon then bloodshed and violence are going to happen in South Africa almost inevitably. A people can take only so much and no more. The history of your own people which I referred to earlier demonstrated this, Vietnam has shown this, the struggle against Portugal has shown this . . . A people made desperate by despair, injustice and oppression will use desperate means.[7]

By 1976, apartheid was at its peak and there was considerable domestic unrest in South Africa, social tension that had been bottled up for years since the legislative acceptance of apartheid and the laws that made it possible in 1948. Thus, in order to understand Tutu's life, which after all was an ongoing personal confrontation with apartheid in the name of God, one must understand the historical development of apartheid.[8]

The heresy of apartheid

Apartheid means 'separateness' in the Afrikaans language, and socially meant a complete separation between Whites and others, be they African, Coloured or Indian. The political enactment of apartheid took place after 1948, when the National Party (NP) won the South African elections and its policy of separation became national policy until the early 1990s. The architect of apartheid was Dr H. F. Verwoerd, Minister of Native Affairs (1951–8) and later Prime Minister (1958–66). However, the social separation coincides with a long history of social segregation going back to the nineteenth century and related to the increasing division of labour following the discovery and exploitation of South Africa's mineral resources.[9] In 1910, the British government passed legislation that unified the Afrikaner republics and the British colonies, but only a small number of Black Africans from the province of the Cape were allowed to vote within the newly constituted South Africa. In 1912, the Black Africans formed the South African Native National Congress that later became the African National Congress (ANC).[10]

The NP enforced the Population Registration Act of 1951, by which all South Africans were classified by race: European (White), Native (Bantu/African), Coloured and Indian (Asian). This typology of social separation dictated where individuals lived, where they worked, the education they received, whom they could marry and where they could be buried. Spatial arrangements took place so as to provide social segregation marked 'Whites only'. Together with this social separation there was the exclusion of non-Whites from economic or political power, while the so-called Coloureds or Indians had more privileges than Africans/Blacks/Natives. South African land was divided according to migration and labour, allocating 87 per cent to Whites and 13 per cent to the so-called Bantu homelands. Within the 'Bantustans', customary law was upheld, regardless of the people's choice, and the only Africans who could move across borders were those needed for White labour, so that the location of one's birth, 15 years of residency or ten years' continuous employment for the same employer allowed people to claim residency in a particular area of South Africa.

South Africa became a police state because large police forces were needed to control the different populations; within that police control, all those who challenged the status quo were considered Communists and dealt with by the legislation of apartheid. However, in 1955 the ANC, together with other groups, formed the Congress of the People, which declared a freedom charter at Klipfontein in which was proclaimed a South Africa for all. Later, in 1959, the Pan-African Congress (PAC) was formed as a protest against the Congress of the People, arguing that Whites and Indians were still trying to suppress the voice of Black Africans. The PAC called for peaceful demonstrations, and in March 1960, at Sharpeville, police killed 67 Black Africans and wounded 200 other protestors in what became known as the Sharpeville Massacre. The government banned the existence of the ANC and the PAC.

After the Sharpeville Massacre the government moved between three and four million Black Africans from the White areas into ten ethnically defined homelands. By 1976, residents of some of the ethnic areas had been stripped of their South African nationality and acquired some sort of self-rule. Those areas included Bophuthatswana, Venda and Ciskei.

Challenges to the absolute control of the South African government did exist, and in 1969 the founding of the Black Consciousness Movement, building 'black pride, self-reliance, and defiance in the face of State oppression', was one of them.[11] Students were particularly involved in the larger movement, and in 1969 the foundation of the South African Students' Organization (SASO), with Stephen Bantu Biko, a medical student, as its president, provided an initial social framework for protest.[12] Although leaders faced imprisonment and violence, the movement grew, and in 1972 another organization, the Black People's Convention (BPC), was founded. Biko didn't face prison like the other leaders, but he testified on their behalf and was arrested on 18 August 1977, near Grahamstown in the Eastern Cape.

On the following day Biko was handed to the security police in Port Elizabeth. He was kept naked in a cell until his interrogation began on 6 September. The next day he had to be moved to Pretoria with head injuries and was transported, again naked, in a police van. He died on 12 September. His death focused international attention on the South African regime, and the United Nations Security Council imposed an arms embargo, the first in the history of the UN. Biko's funeral took place in King William's Town in the Eastern Cape on 25 September, attended by 15,000 people, including diplomatic delegations from the USA and several Western countries. Desmond Tutu, then Bishop of Lesotho, was one of the speakers, and he spoke of Jesus the liberator, who was killed on a cross, and appealed to White Christians to show solidarity, convinced that the God of Jesus wanted a united country in which all were to live in peace. In his words:

> There is no doubt whatsoever that freedom is coming. Yes, it may be a costly struggle still. The darkest hour, they say, is before the dawn. We are experiencing the birth pangs of a new South Africa, a free South Africa, where all of us, black and white together, will walk tall; where all of us, black and white together, will hold hands as we stride forth on the Freedom March to usher in the new South Africa where people will matter because they are human beings made in the image of God.[13]

There had been workers' strikes in 1972 and 1973, and on 16 June 1976, 10,000 children protested against the imposition of the Afrikaans language in schools. Even on that occasion police fired upon the crowds of children. However, international pressure meant that by the late 1970s trade unions were recognized, passes were abolished and Blacks had the possibility of limited urban rights. The churches were still prominent within the life of South Africans but had not yet spoken as a corporate body.[14]

Contemplation and politics

The role of the churches within South Africa became very prominent with Tutu as General Secretary of the South African Council of Churches (SACC) between 1978 and 1985.[15] The SACC had 20 member-churches and four observer member-churches, and represented 15 million Christians, with the exclusion of the churches that advocated a Whites-only membership.[16] In 1979 the SACC passed a resolution that advocated civil disobedience in response to apartheid laws.[17] Tutu had been deeply touched by a little girl who had explained to him that she lived with her widowed mother and sister. According to the little girl, they had no income whatsoever and when hungry they borrowed food, and when no food was available they filled their stomachs with water.[18] In December 1979 Tutu assessed the situation for the benefit of the Anglican Provincial Synod of South Africa, departing from a reflection on Jesus and his ministry and the prayerful life of Anglican communities, and reaching the following conclusion:

> It is precisely our encounter with Jesus in worship and the sacraments, in Bible reading and meditation, that force us to be concerned about the hungry, about the poor, about the homeless, about the banned and the detained, about the voiceless whose voice we seek to be. How can you say you love God whom you have not seen and hate the brother whom you have? He who loved God must love his brother also.[19]

In June 1980, the SACC asked for a meeting with Prime Minister Botha because of the increasingly tense and deteriorating situation. Children had boycotted classes and church workers involved in schools had been arrested. During May 1980, and in solidarity with them, church leaders marched through Johannesburg in a public display of solidarity that was illegal (it was illegal for anybody to demonstrate in public under South African law). The SACC President, Sam Buti and colleagues met Botha in Pretoria on 7 August 1980. During those meetings Tutu spoke of the churches' love for their country and their goodwill towards the authorities; however, he also expressed openly four demands required to improve the socio-political situation in South Africa: (1) common citizenship for all South Africans; (2) the abolition of the pass laws; (3) a stop to people's removal and uprooting; and (4) the setting up of a uniform educational policy.[20]

By October 1981 Tutu realized that the reforms undertaken by Botha did not lead to a fulfilment of Africans' demands and expectations of equality, and he assessed the opportunity thus lost at a meeting of a study group in Johannesburg. However, Tutu remarked that it was very clear from the ruling party elections that there was 'a deeply divided Afrikaner-dom'.[21] At the same time the government announced a commission of enquiry on the SACC finances that would extend to an investigation of all its members. As the SACC did not have state financial support, this was clearly a measure to harass a body that had come to be seen as a danger to the internal security of South Africa. The commission was headed by a Transvaal judge, C. F. Eloff, and Tutu gave evidence in September 1982. In his submission Tutu explained the relation between life and the Scriptures, and how all actions within the life of Christians were judged and reviewed according to the life of Jesus. He went further, in case the South African state were to consider lives within churches as pious actions without socio-political engagement, summarizing some of his previous analysis of the Bible with the following words:

> I have already said we owe our ultimate loyalty and allegiance only to God. With due respect I want to submit that no secular authority nor its appointed commissions has any competence whatsoever to determine how a church is a church, nor what is the nature of the Gospel of Jesus Christ. When secular authority tries to do this then it is usurping divine prerogatives and the prerogatives of the Church itself.[22]

In August 1984, the South African Parliament incorporated Asians and Coloured members but still rejected the possibility of Black Africans having parliamentary rights. In February 1983, Tutu had spoken at the University of Cape Town of his sense of exclusion. He now argued that once again Blacks were treated as strangers, as if they did not exist; however, he was of the opinion that even had they been invited to take their places in the chamber, they would not have accepted because the reforms did not go far enough and still the majority were excluded from the life of South Africa as a nation.[23] By 1983, the Black opposition groups had converged into a United Democratic Front, still seen as a political manifestation of the ANC. Unrest grew as South Africa became involved in wars outside its borders, and the general sense was that neither the government nor the opposition had enough political power to solve the political turmoil. There was violence and protest at the August 1984 reforms, and the biggest strike in the history of South Africa took place on 4 and 5 November 1984. In December, Tutu delivered the Nobel Lecture in Norway, accepting a Nobel Prize for Peace, and ended with a global call to foster peace and harmony, saying: 'Let us work to be peacemakers, those given a wonderful share in our Lord's ministry of reconciliation. If we want peace, so we have been told, let us work for justice. Let us beat our swords into ploughshares.'[24]

During 1985, South Africa faced a financial crisis as banks, led by the US Chase Manhattan Bank, decided not to extend loans to it. There were further talks of reforms, and even bankers went abroad to talk to the leadership of the ANC in exile. Violence against informants of the regime claimed lives, and Tutu urged people not to use it. In October, and already as Bishop of Johannesburg, he addressed the Political Committee of the United Nations General Assembly in New York. His exposition was very clear, explaining his own situation to the international community:

> I am a Bishop in the Church of God. I am fifty-four years old. I am a Nobel laureate. Many would say I am reasonably responsible. In the land of my birth I cannot vote. An eighteen-year-old, because he or she is white (or since August last year so-called Coloured or Indian), can.[25]

In April 1986, a body from the diocese of Cape Town met in order to finalize the election of a successor to Archbishop Philip Russell, leader of all Anglicans in South Africa, who was retiring. As Tutu was one of the possible candidates he was asked to speak about his view of different matters related to the Church, and of course about the challenges of contemporary politics in a segregated South Africa. His appraisal of the situation was realistic and moving:

> I have no hope of real change from this government unless they are forced. We face a catastrophe in this land and only the action of the international community by applying pressure can save us. Our children are dying. Our land is burning and bleeding and so I call the international community to apply punitive sanctions against this government to help us establish a new South Africa – non-racial, democratic, participatory and just. This is a non-violent strategy to help us do so.[26]

Despite Tutu's call for sanctions, he was chosen as the new Archbishop of Cape Town and ex-officio was the leader of Anglicans in South Africa, Lesotho, Mozambique, Namibia, Swaziland and the island of St Helena. On 7 September 1986 he was publicly welcomed to St George's Cathedral in Cape Town, and he delivered a sermon stressing the centrality of spiritual realities within a deteriorating South African situation, in which 25,000 people would be detained between June and December 1986 and 1,300 would die due to political violence that year alone.[27] He asked for the Eucharist to be celebrated daily in every parish of the archdiocese, for people to go on retreats, for fasting, for scriptural reading, for a Christian life that would enforce attitudes of communion within South African society. He told the congregation:

> I am reiterating calls that have been made before. Could we for instance, as we choose to fast corporately on Fridays, agree to pray especially on that day for our Republic of South Africa that injustice and oppression and unjust rule will end and that God's righteousness, love, peace and reconciliation will prevail?[28]

On 24 February 1988, the South African government outlawed 17 anti-apartheid organizations. Violence escalated. Already the previous year Tutu, during a visit to Maputo, had stressed the possibility of martyrdom and the fact that at one point or another the use of violence against an unjust regime was justified. On 29 February, church leaders met at Cape Town and marched, arms linked, towards the Parliament building, an action that was of course illegal under South African law. They numbered 150, and as they faced a police contingent they knelt and sang hymns.[29] The police arrested the leaders and used water cannon to disperse the rest, ending the day with mass arrests, while the foreign media quickly reported that a new era had begun as church leaders took to the streets to protest against the regime. Church leaders later called for a protest rally on 13 March 1988, which was banned by the government. They then called for an interfaith meeting on 12 March, at which Tutu spoke very strong words:

> I finish, my friends, by saying: if they want to take on the Church of God, I warn them. Read a little bit of history and see what happened to those who tried to take on the Church of God. Don't read all of history. Just read your own history. I just warn them that even if they were to remove this, that, or the other person, the Church of God will stay.[30]

In 1989, President P. W. Botha resigned and there were hopes that a negotiated settlement could be reached, particularly because the public protests were increasing, and ambassadors from 12 European nations had met with church leaders and were putting ever more pressure on the South African government to comply with international standards of equality, law and finances. In February 1990, the new President, F. W. de Klerk, proclaimed the end of apartheid, authorized the existence of the ANC and the PAC, and released Nelson Mandela, who since his arrest in 1962 had been political prisoner number one for 27 years. Despite the increasing degree of violence, South Africa held its first democratic and non-racial elections in April 1994, with the election of Nelson Mandela as President of South Africa in a coalition that included the NP and the Zulu Inkatha Freedom Party (IFP). Later, on 8 May 1996, South Africa adopted a post-apartheid constitution recognizing the equal rights of all South Africans. This omitted any mention of group rights or any provincial autonomy that could create any social difference between different races in the new democratic South Africa. As a result of this constitutional development, the NP left the government coalition. However, Desmond Tutu remained one of those advocating a new South Africa of common equality, which had to face its past and years of discrimination and violence. Thus, Tutu became central to the idea of a Truth and Reconciliation Commission (TRC) that required, in cases of major atrocities, a public confession of guilt in order to acquire forgiveness from the state. This constituted a unique view of retributive law within the international community.[31]

The South African TRC

The TRC operated from 1995 to 2001, and following the mandate provided by the 1993 Constitution (Act Number 200) and the 1995 National Unity and Reconciliation Act (Number 34, 26 July 1995), it put a heavy emphasis on reconciliation, nation building and a culture of human rights. The figure of Archbishop Desmond Tutu was central to such an exercise, because unlike the work of TRCs in other countries, less emphasis was given to legal retribution and punitive justice and more to the process of reconciliation.[32] The following paragraph in Act 34 of 1995 sets up the whole mandate of the TRC:

> To provide for the investigation and the establishment of as complete a picture as possible of the nature, causes and extent of gross violations of human rights committed during the period from 1 March 1960 to the cut-off date contemplated in

the Constitution,[33] within or outside the Republic, emanating from the conflicts of the past, and the fate or whereabouts of the victims of such violations; the granting of amnesty to persons who make full disclosure of all the relevant facts relating to acts associated with a political objective committed in the course of the conflicts of the past during the said period; affording victims an opportunity to relate the violations they suffered; the taking of measures aimed at the granting of reparation to, and the rehabilitation and the restoration of the human and civil dignity of, victims of violations of human rights; reporting to the Nation about such violations and victims; the making of recommendations aimed at the prevention of the commission of gross violations of human rights; and for the said purposes to provide for the establishment of a Truth and Reconciliation Commission, a Committee on Human Rights Violations, a Committee on Amnesty and a Committee on Reparation and Rehabilitation; and to confer certain powers on, assign certain functions to and impose certain duties upon that Commission and those Committees; and to provide for matters connected therewith.[34]

In practice, and within the works of the South African TRC, the idea of a national reconciliation and the centrality of a human being's justice through truth overtook any idea of legal reparation or the accountability of the witnesses in a court of law; indeed, there were complaints about the public manipulation of personal narratives by the perpetrators of human rights abuses, accusing some of adapting their narratives so that a legal pardon for their crimes might be possible.[35] The numbers of those applications for amnesty were larger than anticipated – the Amnesty Committee was unprepared for the 7,046 applications it had received by May 1997, the cut-off date.[36]

Unlike the total privacy granted by the Chilean TRC, the South African 1995 Act required 'gross human rights violations' to be heard in public.[37] The TRC classified 20 per cent of all applications within this realm of 'gross' and therefore 'public'. Among the 20,000 testimonies by victims of state repression, only some that involved large numbers of people were heard publicly, because otherwise most of the time of the commissioners would have been taken up with public hearings, broadcast on television, concerned with human rights abuses. But the public hearings had a cathartic national impact, and the forceful but fatherly figure of an embracing Desmond Tutu dominated the proceedings, so that it is possible to argue that without Tutu's moral authority and all-embracing attitude, some of the proceedings would never have had the impact they had on nation-building and reconciliation. For Archbishop Tutu was very blunt and clear in stating his sense of forgiveness and reconciliation:

> True forgiveness deals with the past, all of the past, to make the future possible. We cannot go on nursing grudges even vicariously for those who cannot speak for themselves any longer. We have to accept that what we do we do for generations past, present, and yet to come. That is what makes a community a community or a people a people – for better or for worse.[38]

If the Chilean TRC had no powers to take legal action regarding the testimonies of victims and perpetrators, the South African TRC had powers to assert the social truth, to investigate testimonies and to act as a court of law by providing a legal closure and the application of amnesty, and thus legal pardon, to those who had been perpetrators of human rights abuses and had cooperated with the TRC. According to Graeme Simpson, the danger inherent within this amnesty was clear: 'there is a real possibility that the TRC, by granting amnesty to confessed killers, may actually have contributed to the sense of impunity that fuels the burgeoning rate of violent crime'.[39] Nevertheless, the powers of prosecution/immunity were certainly indigenized by the fact that Archbishop Tutu insisted on the importance of an African sense of community, justice, retribution, truth and reconciliation, recalling a concept used by several African groups: *ubuntu*.[40]

Ubuntu refers to 'an expression of community, representing a romanticized vision of "the rural African community" based upon reciprocity, respect for human dignity, community co-

hesion and solidarity'.[41] The concept was invoked in the 1993
Interim Constitution, and in Constitutional Court judgements,
and challenged the patience of some trained barristers who
were advocating and sustaining the application of a universal
sense of human rights and the compliance by the South African
state with international law and international treatises. Archbishop Tutu's presence at the public hearings prevailed, and
while the amnesty provisions of the 1995 Act were applied, it
was the reconciliation and nation-building in the public sphere
through Tutu's reflection on *ubuntu* that made the headlines
and even questioned if legal and criminal retribution was the
answer to problems of justice, peace and state violence.[42]

The critics of the South African TRC were many; in reality,
South Africa was able to come out of a despicable period of
institutional racism and state repression because the TRC,
while unable to cope with all the tasks assigned to it, combined
all legal, political and philosophical aspects of the past, the
present and the future of the South African state. Desmond
Tutu had a lot to do with that national success.

However, for those who may have thought that the
Archbishop of Cape Town was a politician, one must state
clearly that Tutu reached decisions on his public, social and
ecclesial conduct through the daily celebration of the Eucharist,
through the constant reading of the Scriptures and long
hours contemplating the life and attitudes of Jesus within the
Gospels. It was that continuous contemplation of God and his
actions that made him available for the Christians of South
Africa, and without those intense moments of contemplation
he would probably not have acted in the same way. In an interview with journalists on 2 February 1990, he was very clear in
stating that 'religion has a relevance for the whole of life and we
have to say whether a particular policy is consistent with the
policy of Jesus Christ or not, and if you want to say that that is
political, then I will be a politician in those terms'.[43]

In the following chapter I explore the life of Mother Teresa
of Calcutta, another person who challenged the effects of

political policies on the poorest of society and the unborn, by operating herself a parallel social world driven by her contemplation of God and the face of God reflected among the poorest of society.

6

Mother Teresa of Calcutta

———◆◆◆———

Mother Teresa of Calcutta (1910–97) remains one of the most revered icons of twentieth-century Christianity for Christians and non-Christians alike. Her social iconic power lies not only in the charitable work that she carried out single-handed but in her public declarations against Western policies related to abortion, euthanasia and economic profit. For many, she was an example of holiness, of a direct personal and religious connection to the divine that many would have liked to achieve but were not ready to embrace in their lifestyles. For others, she went too far because she tried to tell political powers how to transform society through religious commitment, something that is anathema for a secularized and profit-making society. This chapter examines the life and work of the founder of the Missionaries of Charity and her own practice of contemplation and politics in the contemporary world. She remains a forceful image of the God who preferred the poor and the marginalized, and a model of prayer and activism for Christians today.

A determined life

In 1995, Christopher Hitchens, the Washington-based writer of the 'Culture elite' column for *Vanity Fair*, wrote a cynical book bearing the title *The Missionary Position* that asked questions about Mother Teresa and her involvement in contemporary politics. The book does not rank among the most inspiring regarding ways of committing oneself to the poor of this world, but it does reflect the anger and distrust of the secular world towards a religious figure who went too far. For Hitchens, Mother Teresa was not to be trusted because she met with dictators, tycoons and convicted fraudsters, and in many cases accepted help from them. Further, Hitchens questioned her opinions on matters of sexuality and her function as a publicity agent on behalf of the Catholic Church. He concluded that 'She has herself purposely blurred the supposed distinction between the sacred and the profane, to say nothing of the line that separates the sublime from the ridiculous. It is past time that she was subjected to the rational critique that she has evaded so arrogantly and for so long.'[1]

Hitchens, who had written other books unveiling political and social scandals, was not pleased with the assurance that Mother Teresa brought to other people and the indirect support that she lent to more conservative Christian groups within the politics of the USA. If Hitchens failed to understand the freedom of Mother Teresa, not bound by a political system, it was because the politics of this contemplative cannot be understood without looking at the historical development of a Christian who took the life of God and of others very seriously, becoming herself a human sign of the divine contradictions within contemporary society.

Mother Teresa was born Agnes Gonxha Bojaxhiu on 27 August 1910, in Skopje (at that time Üsküp), capital of Macedonia, a town that was part of the Turkish empire. She came from an Albanian family and considered herself throughout her life an Albanian. She was the youngest child of Nikola and Drane Bojaxhiu, and followed the birth of Aga in 1904 and Lazar in 1907. She received her first Holy Communion at the age of five and a half, and was confirmed at six, in November 1916. Her father died when she was eight, and the family found life difficult economically. However, they grew very close to the Jesuit Parish of the Sacred Heart, where Agnes, at the early age of 12, felt that God was calling her to the religious missionary life. The family prayed every evening, went to church every day, prayed a daily rosary and assisted in the ritual service of the Virgin Mary. During the summer holidays they made the pilgrimage to Letnice, where the Virgin Mary was venerated. At the age of 18, in September 1928, she joined the Institute of the Blessed Virgin Mary (known as the Sisters of Loreto), an Irish missionary religious congregation with missions in India. After some training in Dublin she received the name Sister Mary Teresa (after St Thérèse of Lisieux), and in December 1928 was sent to India, arriving in Calcutta on 6 January 1929. She took her first vows in May 1931, and was assigned to the Loreto Entally community in Calcutta, where she taught at St Mary's High School for girls from 1931 to 1948. In 1944 she became the school's principal.

It was on 10 September 1946, and on the train from Calcutta to Darjeeling, where she was to have her yearly retreat, that Mother Teresa remembered having a 'call within a call' – she felt directly called to serve the most destitute of Indian society.[2] She had witnessed enormous poverty in Calcutta, most of it just outside the convent walls, and after a time of discernment she was granted permission to leave the convent and work among the poor of Calcutta. On 17 August 1948, she dressed for the first time in a white, blue-bordered sari and crossed the gates of the convent on her road to serve the poor. After a short course with the Medical Mission Sisters in Patna, Mother Teresa found a place to stay with the Little Sisters of the Poor, and on 21 December 1948 she visited the slums for the first time. Her first experience was visiting families, washing children, caring for an old man on the road and nursing a woman suffering from hunger and tuberculosis. Her daily routine was clear: she took part in the Eucharist and then, rosary in hand, went to meet those who needed her most. First she started an open-air school for children that lived in a slum of Calcutta, where some volunteers joined her. All of them had been her own students and they allowed her to seek for 'the unwanted, the unloved and the uncared for'. It was on 19 March 1949 that the first volunteer, Agnes, joined her, and another 15 volunteers joined her in the following 12 months. With the financial help of private benefactors she extended her charitable work.

During 1949 she took Indian nationality, binding her own future to the poor of India, and decided to start her own religious community. The foundation of a new religious congregation was prepared by writing a draft constitution, work undertaken by Mother Teresa with the help of the Jesuits Fr Julien Henry, Fr Celest Van Exem, and Fr P. De Gheldere. On 7 October 1950 – the feast of the Holy Rosary – the Vatican granted permission for her to start a new religious order, the Missionaries of Charity, to look after those society had rejected and those not looked after by others within the Archdiocese of Calcutta. On that day the Archbishop of Calcutta celebrated the Eucharist in the presence of 12 Missionary Sisters of Charity and Fr Van Exem read the papers of foundation. The Missionaries of Charity took the usual religious vows of poverty, chastity and obedience, with the addition of a fourth vow: the service of the poorest of the poor. The aims of the new religious congregation were the spreading of the gospel for their salvation and the sanctification of the poor. The first religious house, later to become the Mother House of the Missionaries of Charity, was sold to Mother Teresa by a Muslim who was moving to Pakistan, and was located at Lower Circular Road, Calcutta.

The religious task was very poignant in a stratified society such as India, where the system of caste within Hinduism had at different times labelled groups of people within society as 'unclean and undesirable'. That was the case of the untouchables and those unwanted by their families, either because of illness or ritual pollution. By the early 1960s, Mother Teresa had started sending sisters to other parts of India, and in February 1965, Pope Paul VI recognized the important contribution that the Missionaries of Charity had made to the care of the poor by decreeing that Mother Teresa's religious family could become an international congregation rather than a diocesan group of helpers to the local bishop. The first foundation outside India was in Venezuela, followed by Rome and Tanzania. By the 1980s, Mother Teresa had opened houses in almost all of the countries of the Eastern Bloc, including the Soviet Union, Albania and Cuba.

Previously, in 1963, Mother Teresa had founded the Missionaries of Charity Brothers, and had established an important distinction between the active and the contemplative branches of her own congregation. In 1979 she started the brothers' contemplative branch, with Father Sebastian Vazhakala as superior, and in 1984 a new religious family for priests was incorporated – the Missionaries of Charity Fathers. She also incorporated lay people and co-workers into her family through the foundation of the Co-Workers of Mother Teresa and the Sick and Suffering Co-Workers – people of many faiths and nationalities together with whom she shared the values of prayer, simplicity, sacrifice and her apostolate of humble works. Later, a new group was formed under the umbrella of the Lay Missionaries of Charity. For priests who wanted to share her search for simplicity she founded the Corpus Christi Movement for Priests. There is no doubt that while the Missionaries of Charity's sisters are the most well known of her religious family, all the other branches provide a significant support for the care of the most destitute within society.

Her pastoral work has been widely recognized by established international organizations and she received the following prizes, among others: Pope John XXIII Peace Prize (1971), Nehru Prize for her promotion of international peace and understanding (1972), Balzan Prize (1979), Nobel Prize (1979), the US Presidential Medal of Freedom (1985) plus the Templeton Prize (1973), the Indian Padmashari (1962) and the Magsaysay awards. Mother Teresa received all of them, in her words, 'for the glory of God and in the name of the poor'.

By the 1990s her health had become frail, and while she continued running her religious family, in March 1997 she confirmed her newly appointed successor, Sister M. Nirmala Joshi MC, as superior general of the Missionaries of Charity. She died of a heart attack on 5 September 1997, and was given a state funeral by the government of India. Her body was buried at the Mother House of the Missionaries of Charity. After her death there were widespread calls for her process of canonization (the road to recognized sainthood within the Catholic Church) to be opened, and only two years after her death Pope John Paul II agreed to the opening of her Cause for Canonization. On 20 December 2002, John Paul II approved the decrees of her heroic virtues and miracles, recognizing one of the outstanding examples of Christian holiness of the twentieth century. By the time of her death, the Missionaries of Charity numbered 4,000, working in 610 foundations spread throughout 123 countries.

A life of contemplation

Mother Teresa spoke of a personal vision of the Christ while on a train to Darjeeling in 1946, and of a year in which she felt close to God and had the opportunity of unfolding God's plan for her and her group of associates. One of her strengths was the intensity of prayer and the abundant time given to piety and personal prayer. She ingrained such practices in the Missionaries of Charity, who in their daily life pray at all times, have very little recreation, sleep or food. The centre of Mother Teresa's contemplative moment was the daily celebration of the Eucharist – a moment of adoration and contemplation rather than a creative liturgical moment. The morning and evening prayers were always complemented by a requirement to pray at all times, be it the rosary, the self-composed prayers or the *Salve*. Those who journeyed with her and stayed at her communities always found it difficult to follow the communal prayers that mark the whole day and take place at all times, interrupted only by service to the poor, the eating of food and a few hours of sleep.

It was in the practice of constant prayer, manual work and simplicity that Mother Teresa's practice of community resembled that of ancient monastic life rather than the life of contemporary religious communities. A present-day community, while serving others, requires communal reflection and planning to understand and foster its internal individual relationships. Mother Teresa placed the Eucharist and the Blessed Sacrament at the centre of life, and contemplation and other communal activities became secondary in a scale of daily needs. It is possible, therefore, to suggest that she was a contemplative in action, who could not function without that constant struggle with the God of life. The God of Mother Teresa was a compassionate but personal God who challenged her all her life and made her grow through experiences of despair and doubt. Indeed, Mother Teresa described doubts about God that were present for 50 years of her life. While she was in hospital in 1997, the Archbishop of Calcutta, Henry D'Souza, performed an exorcism by way of prayer over her because she was extremely restless and agitated at night.

She summarized the ascent to God in a constant search for peace – individual, communal, social and global. That search for peace required six clear consecutive steps: silence, prayer, faith, love, service and finally peace. The call to every human being was to perform small actions of service and love to others, and to pray for peace, in whatever tradition the person had been raised. She prayed with Hindus, Muslims and those of other religions, and even with those who only believed in God and not in the Christ of Christianity. Those non-Christians she exhorted to pray by replacing the name of Jesus with the name of God. Like many other Catholic missionaries, she encouraged the Hindu practices of meditation and a simple life, as followed in the Indian ashrams, spirituality that was popularized outside India through the writings of the Indian Jesuit Anthony de Mello, particularly his book on the path to God, *Sadhana*.

The hagiographic image of a saintly maiden who never has a problem is not the reality of a holy person, who is always open to God's will and who struggles in a very personal manner with the God whom she contemplates. While continuous prayer offers a verbal petition to God for the needs of the world, the contemplative is the one who, by constancy, achieves a close and personal relationship with God and is pushed by him to be an instrument within society, even during times and situations that the contemplative does not want or does not enjoy. The ascent of the mystic is a lonely moment of direct personal encounter between the human and the divine, with unforeseen consequences and a good deal of pain, as well as consolation. It is that side of Mother Teresa that allowed her to speak to society by works and words, without fear of loneliness or rejection. The contemplative experiences the loneliness and the consolation of the mountain, where only a few come face to face with God in silence and solitude. In that sense, the contemplative is a courageous and lonely person who has found a higher realm of engagement and who while in contemplation does not see danger but welcomes the possibility of alleviating pain and suffering in this world and the next.

A political life

If one returns to the criticisms made by Christopher Hitchens, it is understandable that Mother Teresa annoyed many of those who perceived the practice of religion as the practice of good works for the poor (charity) but without any challenge to society. The same had already happened with the theology of liberation that had been deemed by the US administration as unsuitable and 'communist' because the theologians of liberation had asked questions about the social conditions of the poor and the political reasons for their poverty. Mother Teresa created the same contradiction: she was loved by public figures such as President Reagan, but suspected of going too far by those who wanted to keep religion and politics as separate ways of being in society.

It was in 1969 that she started to become a public figure, when Malcolm Muggeridge made a hagiographic film about her life and publicized her work through his book *Something Beautiful for God*.[3] The impact of that initial media exercise was enormous at a time when the post-Second Vatican Council Catholic Church was looking for human signs of renewal. As a result of Muggeridge's work, Mother Teresa became a clear symbol of interfaith renewal and Christian commitment amid the 1960s revolution and the subsequent loss of Christian values within Western society. That image of the unchangeable message of an unchangeable Church was supported by the Vatican, without its realizing that Mother Teresa had more inclusive ideas for society; indeed, she followed with excitement the concept of the 'people of God' as an all-inclusive way of understanding God's love for all. Although conservative in her ideas of social morality, she was quite advanced in her political ideas of diversity and social inclusion, a point that was missed in Christian American conservative circles and by the media of Washington, DC.[4]

Her meetings with international politicians, some of whom were hated, were always controversial. However, Mother Teresa accepted them in the name of the poor as those meetings helped her to outline the sufferings of the poor and the unwanted through the international media. For example, in 1981 she received the *Légion d'honneur* from the government of Haiti, and appeared in a controversial picture with Michele Duvalier, wife of the Haitian dictator Jean-Claude 'Baby Doc' Duvalier. She also received the Integrity Award from John-Roger, leader of the Movement for Spiritual Inner Awareness (MSIA), together with a cheque for $10,000. She regularly visited Charles Keating of Lincoln Savings and Loan, a man who gave her more than one million dollars in donations – when Keating was later imprisoned for fraud, Mother Teresa wrote to Judge Lance Ito requesting leniency.

In 1985, President Ronald Reagan conferred on Mother Teresa the US Presidential Medal of Freedom. She could not receive her medal with the other 12 nominees because of other commitments, but received it in the Rose Garden of the White House on her own. President Reagan remarked that:

> Only one of the recipients could not attend because she had work to do – not special work, not unusual work for her, but everyday work which is both special and urgent in its own right. Mother Teresa was busy, as usual, saving the world. And I mean that quite literally.[5]

The Medal of Freedom, given to those who have served the USA, was given to Mother Teresa because, according to Reagan, 'the goodness in some hearts transcends all borders and all narrow nationalistic considerations. Some people, some very few people are, in the truest sense, citizens of the world.' There came a moment during the presentation when Reagan mentioned that perhaps Mother Teresa would not be keeping the actual medal for herself: 'May I say that this is the first time I've given the Medal of Freedom with the intuition that the recipient might take it home, melt it down and turn it into something that can be sold to help the poor.' Mother Teresa's inclusive speech was contagious. Other pastoral agents within the Catholic Church would have preferred to have no association with President Reagan and his administration's involvement in the wars and human rights abuses that were taking place in Central America. She said in her acceptance speech:

> And you, you cannot go where we go. You cannot do what we do. But together, we are doing something beautiful for God. And my gratitude to you, President, and your family and to your people. It's my prayer for you that you may grow in holiness to this tender love for the poorest of the poor.

As previously argued, it is impossible to disassociate her political actions from her personal religious and Christian contemplation of the God of life. Her intense prayer and intense personal spiritual struggle made her unafraid to seek in the public sphere what she was seeking to achieve in her private sphere. The politics of contemplation quickly became the politics of society and the politics of the public sphere. To that effect there were two particular areas that Mother Teresa addressed in the public sphere: social morality, and the plurality of faith communities. Both were upsetting to a Western secularized society.

Social morality

In receiving many awards and invitations throughout the world, Mother Teresa acquired public platforms from which she was unrelenting in her own critique of Western society and of political systems where there were those who had no one to care for them. For example, she upset the American Bible belt by suggesting that Christ was present in those rejected by society, including those who had contracted HIV/AIDS at a time when a clear association was being made between it and homosexuality and sinfulness and HIV/AIDS. Mother Teresa received lots of coverage in *Time* magazine, where she was reported as saying: 'The dying, the crippled, the mentally ill, the unwanted, the unloved – they are Jesus in disguise . . . [through the] poor people I have an opportunity to be 24 hours a day with Jesus.'[6]

When, in March 1966, Fr Sebastian Vazhakala, superior general of the Missionaries of Charity Brothers, who worked in Rome through the Casa Serena with those rejected by society, expressed his admiration for Mother Teresa's social work, she immediately corrected him. She didn't like the idea that the Missionaries of Charity were social workers, and told him: 'We are not doing social work; this is God's work – because whatever we do to the least of my brothers, that is Jesus' saying – you do to me.'

Mother Teresa managed to incorporate many social contexts and many realities of poverty worldwide. For example, in 1976 she explored the possibility of opening a novitiate of the Missionaries of Charity in Los Angeles, and Fr Vazhakala was entrusted with the first explorations. He could not find the same material poverty as in India, but he found spiritual poverty within the busyness of American life. Thus, the Missionaries of Charity continued tending to the dying but doing it so as to show the love of Christ for those who were no longer part of a productive and busy society. The Missionaries of Charity breached social, ethnic and racial divides by going out to everybody, speaking of forgiveness and love through their own actions. On another occasion Mother Teresa asked helpers to give cigarettes to the dying. That shocked some of them as they expected that a religious sister would forbid smoking at homes for the dying. However, Mother Teresa suggested that a dying person who had been treated worse than an animal on the streets should have the dignity of a person who had the choice of enjoying a last cigarette.

The plurality of faith

Mother Teresa was a devout and faithful Christian but did not pretend to convert others to Christianity, which was one of the reasons the Indian state didn't see her as a threat at a time when most expatriate missionaries had to leave India after independence. Her instructions to her own associates were very clear, never to force the dying to accept Christianity but allowing them to die following their own way of life and their own beliefs:

> If in coming face to face with God we accept Him in our lives, then we are converting. We become a better Hindu, a better Muslim, a better Catholic, a better whatever we are . . . What God is in your mind you must accept.[7]

There is no doubt that for some, those words were challenging. However, her public authority came from her own dedication to people and her own commitment to speak for those who did not have a voice in society. In 1985, she attended the United Nations University of Peace Conference in order to discuss the common bringing of a New World Order based on peace, being present at a meeting that was also attended by Marilyn Ferguson of the New Age movement, Helen Caldicott, president of Physicians for Social Responsibility, an organization that advocated unilateral disarmament, the Dalai Lama and Archbishop Desmond Tutu. Later, in November 1986, she attended the Summit for Peace in Assisi, where members of the main faith traditions of the world prayed for world peace. As expected, her public appearances were revered by some and despised by others.

Contemporary politics

While the Catholic Church has always proclaimed sainthood as a public recognition of virtue and heroism within the Christian life, John Paul II made a significant statement by recognizing many more saints than any Pope before him. The cause of beatification of Mother Teresa ran faster than that of anybody else, and she was beatified on 19 October 2003. In 1999, John Paul II waived the period of five years required before any request for beatification could be filed, and in 2002 recognized the healing of a non-Christian woman in India as a miracle obtained through Mother Teresa's intercession. The woman had a large abdominal tumour that disappeared after the Missionaries of Charity prayed for Mother Teresa's intervention in order to heal her. In 2001, on the Feast of the Assumption of Mary, the diocesan inquiry into her sanctity was closed with a positive result, and it was recognized that many thousands of pilgrims of all faiths witnessed to a cult of the saints at Mother Teresa's tomb. For example, on 26 August 2000, Hindus, Sikhs and Muslims had prayed together at an anniversary celebration of Mother Teresa's birth. Blessed Mother Teresa would need the recognition of another miracle in order to be recognized as a saint, but there is no doubt that her life had triggered the service of many to the poor and the unwanted, regardless of their religious affiliation.

For many, Mother Teresa stands as a pious, dedicated nun who gave her individual self to the poor and those despised by society. For others, such as Christopher Hitchens, Mother Teresa was an unwelcome guest in Western society, and particularly American society. She challenged the established social morality of legal abortion and divorce with her own Christian morality, making and fostering connections to those in governance. Thus, unlike some evangelical Christians, she pleaded in the highest spheres for those who suffer, without condemning modernity or postmodernity as a wicked, sinful way of life. Her politics of religion were the politics of Christian involvement within society, an involvement that arose from her deep contemplation of the divine in the Eucharist. Instead of engaging herself in intellectual and philosophical debates she engaged herself in the practice of love for the poor – thus she fed them, clothed them, cleaned them and gave them a human, dignified place.

Contemplation and politics became one single daily activity for Mother Teresa because the first commandment of loving God and loving one's neighbour was closely articulated in the love of prayer and the love of politics. If God is given praise and love in the soul's contemplation, he is also given praise by the creation of a system of governance that expresses in some way the values of the Kingdom of God: justice, peace and compassion for all – be they friends or enemies, fellow Christians, Muslims or Hindus. In summary, Mother Teresa developed a model of intense daily contemplation of the Incarnation through the presence of God in the Eucharist, while developing a close model of cooperation and prophecy within the international system of political association. For her there was no change without prayer, and no politics without the continuity of the constant contemplation of the creator of all. She was a model of a Christian who didn't disappear into her holiness but became a political activist and an unwanted prophet who nevertheless could not be ignored or sent away. Her authority was the authority of God and her concern was that of those central to Jesus' preaching of the Kingdom of God: the poor and the marginalized.

Mother Teresa took care of bodies as well as souls, and therefore emphasized the importance of the body for salvation and for a Christian involvement in politics, which is the subject of the next chapter.

7

The body and contemplation

In the previous chapter I outlined that Mother Teresa, and with her all Missionaries of Charity, engaged daily in a strenuous control of their bodies through long periods of meditation, prayer and Eucharistic contemplation. In doing so, they became closer to God by spending long periods of time with him, but also they spent long periods of the day with broken and suffering bodies on the streets, in their hospices, orphanages and clinics. Mother Teresa was frail and petite, with a body that didn't conform to the contemporary ideals of care and beauty; however, she used her body as an instrument of God's presence. One could say that her body was an extension of God's body in the world. If God has a body in terms of a planet, as Sallie McFague has rightly suggested, all contemplation of God and his world requires an active participation of the senses and the body, through posture and gesture, for the movement of the soul towards God, with God and on behalf of God.[1] If the involvement of Christians in the world of the social and the political comes out of the celebration of community and the Eucharist (see Chapter 8), the celebration of the Eucharist and any other community activity requires a body that has experienced that moment of intense conversion: the body that surrenders to the vision of the God of all, of the God who is not distant but with oneself in a moment through which nothing else matters and nothing else is important. Bodies do not necessarily have to be sinful and imperfect vehicles of God's action; instead, bodies can be and must be salvific signifiers of God's grace, love and care for humanity.

Contemplative bodies

One of the most significant moments in the history of twentieth-century spirituality and contemplation was the encounter of the Trappist contemplative monk Thomas Merton with Tenzin Gyatso, more commonly known as the Fourteenth Dalai Lama.[2] Merton, who had been allowed to journey to Asia by his Abbot in 1968, was attending a meeting of Catholic contemplative monks in Bangkok, where he was to deliver a lecture to Benedictine contemplatives living in Asia. It was part of a renewal of monastic life that was taking shape after the conclusion of the Second Vatican Council (1962–5), and Merton had decided to visit the Dalai Lama at his home in Dharamsala, India.

The Dalai Lama met with Merton three times during Merton's stay in India, and they discussed the ways of monasticism as well as the possibilities of a Christian–Buddhist dialogue (I have made detailed comments on these meetings in Chapter 1). They were both impressed by each other's knowledge of their different traditions, as well as of their involvement in the renewal and centrality of a contemplative life for the contemporary world. However, one of the central discussions that they recalled in their writings was an exchange they had on the position of the body while in contemplation. For Merton, prayer and contemplation could be conducted in any manner and at any time, while the Dalai Lama was very clear about the lotus position for meditation within Tibetan Buddhism and the fact that the hands were in a particular position. Thus, Merton wrote in his diary: 'He [the Dalai Lama] demonstrated the sitting position for meditation which he said was essential. In the Tibetan meditation posture the right hand (discipline) is above the left (wisdom). In Zen it is the other way around.'[3] For his part, the Dalai Lama wrote: 'He [Thomas Merton] told me a number of things that surprised me, notably that Christian practitioners of meditation do not adopt any particular physical position when they meditate. According to my understanding, position and even breathing are vital.'[4]

It is the preoccupation with posture in meditation that distracts many would-be practitioners, because they are worried about doing the right thing rather than focusing on the object of their contemplation. If the object of contemplation is the mind, the body, the senses, a passage from Scripture, an icon, a word or the Eucharistic presence, the end of every contemplative moment is the possibility of freeing oneself from the secondary things of life, much needed and good, but secondary to the possibility of acquiring freedom of spirit. The humbleness of contemplation requires that a human being free himself or herself from what John Dear calls 'the three factors' that put us apart from the clear message of the Gospels: power, prestige and possessions.[5] In the case of Tibetan Buddhists, the same process takes place in trying to free themselves from the attachment to emotions and things that prevent them from being one with those who suffer and finally exiting the cycle of reincarnation (*samsara*) by means of a constant state of concentration and meditative absorption (*samadhi*).[6]

The discipline of contemplation structured in a monastery through the praying of the daily office, the celebration of the Eucharist and the hours allocated to sleep and work help a person who wants to contemplate, because that person has the desire to locate God at the centrality of life. However, without will and discipline, contemplation could become a series of prayers or recitations in which praise is given to God but the actual necessary silence of the contemplative focused on the contemplated does not take place. For the Dalai Lama, the right hand of discipline is above the left hand of wisdom because it is the discipline of the posture and the hours that aid the will to open the heart and empty the mind in order to leave behind in a continuous movement power, prestige and possessions. Thus, the process of emptying on the one hand and of filling on the other are very similar within all the world religions; it is the contemplative act that becomes central to the lives of those practitioners, regardless of their own traditions and their own ways of facing the same challenges posed by John Dear's 'three factors'.

If one returns to my argument throughout this book, that contemplation and politics have a lot to do with each other, it is possible to argue that Christian life in general should be centred upon prayer, and upon prayer as a service to others. Contemplation as a form of prayer remains the same challenging activity that provides not only the fuel for love of God and neighbour but the structuring of one's activities, relationships and actions within society. The fact is that contemplation has for too long been associated with monasteries and abbeys. That should not be the case any longer, because the commandment to pray and to retreat to a lonely and quiet place is not solely given to contemplative monks or nuns but to all within the Gospels. Jesus spent hours in prayer, particularly in the evening and at night, when he retreated from the daily tasks and daily journeys to converse with God, and to be given a re-affirmation of his mission or, if possible, the opportunity to change a course of action. The structuring of one's daily discipline does not prevent us from having fun or doing whatever we are about to do; instead, the discipline of our lives helps us focus on what is important and necessary and what is not. In a world that assumes spirituality as something important, contemplation has become a fashionable topic.

Take for example the BBC television series *The Monastery*, referred to in the Introduction to this book, in which a group of men allowed themselves time to live in a Benedictine monastery and the television cameras to follow them. They realized that the lives of those who followed the monastic discipline within the English Benedictine Order challenged their own sense of life and their own ideas of the importance of different things within their lives. The act of contemplation challenged them because what is considered a private activity became part of their own lives. This is the paradox of contemplation and bodies: contemplation as an activity of the body is considered private and therefore not accessible to the whole of society, while contemplation has, as any religious activity, a public sphere of influence that is not usually understood. The 'private' activity of contemplating makes individuals, and communities

of those contemplative individuals, question the contemporary
realities and policies of society in a way that public political
activities sometimes do not. The contemplative, by emptying
the body and the mind of the secondary, refills his or her own
existence with the primacy of a transcendent existence that in
turn becomes public. Any contemplative activity that takes
place through an individual's body does not alienate that person from society but instead makes that person more challenging of some of the central preoccupations of other members of
society, lacking in transcendence and consequence and heavily
influenced and pressured by the media and by their social
peers.

Bodies of resistance

The body is needed for prayer, for contemplation and for political action because without the body there would be neither
interaction between a human being and God, between a
human being and another human being nor between a single
human being and a group. In fact, for too long ideas of contemplation have suggested that the spirit lifts towards God as
if separated from the body, while in Christian theology both
body and spirit turn to their Creator God. The former understanding contradicts the central principle of God's action in
the world through the incarnation of his Son, who came as
a human being, suffered on the cross and was raised by his
Father. Indeed, the first conversations about the Resurrection
were not about a metaphysical principle of soul suspension but
about a practical and material problem for the disciples and for
the women who went to the tomb. The women reported to the
disciples that they had gone to the tomb and had not found
the body. Further questions related to the possibility that the
Romans had taken the body and buried it somewhere else.

For if Thomas Merton and the Dalai Lama exchanged views
about meditation and contemplation, they both assumed that
the body was needed in order to prepare that moment of con-

templation and that the disposition of the contemplative was to transcend the materiality of the body in order to connect with the divine. For Merton, the connection with the divine created a social responsibility that embraced other believers' bodies vis-à-vis the realities of the monastery, while for the Dalai Lama the moment of meditation prepared the human subconscious for an attitude of empathy, kindness and understanding on behalf of all sentient beings who were suffering. Thus, the purpose of both acts of contemplation was a relation with a universal principle of goodness, represented in Christianity by a personal encounter with God, and in Tibetan Buddhism by the possibility of renouncing violence, leaving behind possessions and showing kindness to all living beings.

The contemplative body therefore becomes a body of resistance to all values and attitudes that contradict the sign offered by a particular body. The body becomes significant because the body offers itself as symbol, individual and social, of other values, other attitudes, other freedoms. Here is where we reach the central path of understanding of contemplation, the body and the political acts. Here lies the centrality of contemplation not as escapism or personal comfort, but as challenge, as resistance, as elevation, as the higher aim of Christian charity and, in all world religions, as a symbol of freedom from the world.

If one concentrates on Christianity and Buddhism, the paradox arises immediately: a utopia of service and commitment to others is central to both religious traditions, even when Christianity has a central tenet on God and creation while Buddhism does not have a creator God or a monotheistic sense of past, present and future. Thus, the encounter between Thomas Merton and the Fourteenth Dalai Lama is even more important: the encounter of two bodies, two human and contemplative bodies, symbolized the possibility of action arising out of contemplation, meditation, prayer and communion with spiritual realities. For Merton and the Dalai Lama, the need to go beyond the human bodily realities in order to attain a communion with the spiritual did not discard the human body as useless, but emphasized the bodily principle of a divine incarnation and of the body as vehicle and as physical challenge to other materialistic attitudes to life.

The reader might be surprised that I draw parallels between Christian meditation and Buddhist meditation. I am fully aware that the object of desire in contemplation is completely different in Christianity and in Buddhism; however, there is a great difference between Zen Buddhism and Tibetan Buddhism, the kind of Buddhism followed by the Dalai Lama's religious order, the Galugpa (commonly known as the yellow hats because of the magnificent golden head covers they wear in some of their rituals). If a Christian in contemplation relates to God, Christ and the Spirit, a Buddhist monk does not have a belief in a God as creator, but gathers momentum from a self-emptying and a mind-conscious attitude by which he or she can be mindful of the motivation for kindness and the alleviation of suffering that comes out of meditation. Both Christian and Buddhist, however, accept and experience love as a central tenet of their lives, a love that surpasses one's life and one's concerns and that in a utopian manner is understood as contributing to the well-being of others. Christian monastic orders gather in community to pray for the world and its needs; that is, for the well-being of other human beings unknown personally to them. In the case of Buddhists, and particularly Tibetan Buddhists, they meditate in order to free themselves of their passions and selfish attitudes and to achieve enlightenment and exit the chain of suffering. Surprisingly enough, the Dalai Lama and some of the enlightened teachers and monks achieve a state of enlightenment, but decide of their own accord to return to the human world of bodies in order to care for other human beings, to instruct them and also to care for the well-being of all sentient beings.

If one steps back for a moment to take stock of what prayer and the commandment to pray at all times could be about, one realizes that prayer as a communication with the divine and contemplation as an act of communion and love do not assume a selfish attitude of personal salvation. On the contrary, prayer brings out the best in us, and brings us closer to God and his values; it is only by prayer that we then continue walking on the Christian path and in the ways of the Gospels. Contemplative bodies are transformed into bodies of resistance to John Dear's 'three factors': power, prestige and possessions.[7]

Bodies of inclusion

One of the most problematic faces of a contemporary forceful Christianity, sometimes experienced by converts, is the temptation to exclude others, while at the same time focusing on prayer and contemplation as tools for fighting against 'a sinful and destitute world'. Theological thinking that has divided Christians and the world has stressed the metaphorical distinctions used generally by John's Gospel, choosing to reject the more socio-political description of Jesus' life as portrayed in the Gospels of Mark and Luke. This is not the place to go into those differences, but rather to challenge Christian attitudes that exclude the salvific value of God's work, God's love and the Incarnation as a principle of cross–resurrection–salvation.

God loves the world and he loves all, particularly the sinner. It is to that divine life that the contemplative turns in order to learn, to love and to embrace. It is the moments or hours spent in contemplation of God's attributes and action in history that make a Christian into a contemplative. It is the joy of the simplicity of God that makes a Christian loving towards others and inclusive towards all, because God himself has welcomed us into his own universal love. Doctrinally, all creeds, councils and ways of being Christian come out of the commandment to love God and to love neighbour. Attitudes of exclusion have to be experienced through the same lens of inner contemplation of God, who loved the world and sent his Son to redeem all – not some, not the learned or the clever, but all.

If I return once again to Thomas Merton and the Fourteenth Dalai Lama, their lives have touched others because of their sense of personal holiness through not only their free choice of a way of life in which God or the spiritual realm is at the centre, but also because they were open to the exploration of other people's beliefs and lives, not solely out of personal curiosity but out of their sense that every human being is recipient of some divine love and some divine inspiration. It is that belief in human beings that allows contemporary holy people to embody the reality of the divine and make it tangible. Within the frailty of Mother Teresa or the vulnerability of Sheila Cassidy one can see glimpses of the divinity who cares for this world and for all human beings and all sentient beings, in the language of the Dalai Lama.

Thus, three levels of inclusion, as extensions of the loving body of God, are important for the development of a contemplative Christian body: inclusion of strangers, inclusion of other beliefs and inclusion of politics as diversity. In expanding on these three extensions of the body of God and of the Christian contemplative body of Christ, I recognize that my theological understanding of Christianity is inclusivist. As a theologian and as a Christian, I assume my intellectual and personal limitations: it is God's world that we live in and it is to him that we shall return. Thus, God's salvific plan is known to us, but we must recognize our limitations in interpretation and understanding so as to suggest that it is ultimately God's plan and God's planet that we are dealing with. He may have plans and intentions that we cannot comprehend, and as we have seen through many reforms throughout the history of the universal Church, there is a diversity of understandings about what God wants of the Church and what God intends to do through his vehicles of salvation.

It is from that sobering statement that the three levels of inclusion arise. There are many people who are not part of our local communities, and many strangers who have other religious beliefs and other political ideas with whom we share our daily lives or whom we see represented in the news and in national and international responses by our governments and our churches today. It is to them that the central tenet of our

Christian faith extends: love God and love others because God loves them.

Strange bodies and Christian inclusion

I have lived outside my native Chile for 27 years, in Europe, in Africa and most of the time in the UK. Throughout these years there has been a decline in the numbers of those attending church services on Sunday; however, there has not been a decline in spirituality and the search for spiritual practices. Yes, a decline in church attendance, but not a decline in charity work, donations to charity and generous responses to the plight of victims of natural disasters, such as the 2004 tsunami, refugees or those without shelter, food or clean water in other parts of the world.

It cannot be said that vocations to the ordained ministry are on the increase, but it seems that retreat centres, prayer houses and spiritual direction are not activities that one could consider to be declining. The universal Church is growing in numbers elsewhere, though it seems that the European decline is here to stay. I am not strongly concerned about this because the massification of religion creates other problems. I am more concerned that our own smaller communities have the possibility of loving God, of experiencing prayer and meditation, of feeling themselves real instruments of God's grace in contemporary society. It is through those communities that the body of Christ, made of many individual bodies, will arise as a sign of love and inclusion within society.

The media plays endlessly with the possibilities of difference and change in society that people different from us bring to our communities and our lives. However, strange bodies, be they immigrants or believers from other religious traditions, bring to us the possibility of opening ourselves to the wonders of God, who embraces all and gives life to all. The fear of a stranger assumes the danger of misunderstanding and of a lack of social communication. What makes that nonsense is that when we go to other countries and are in other situations, we realize how human beings share something in common if we search for that commonality and if we are open to recognize God in the stranger. It is through daily moments of conversation and intimacy with God that we take stock of a Christianity that is universal, globalized and that shows the action and love of God in many different parts of the world and through many different peoples. To welcome the stranger remains part of a Christian activity in which we recognize the primacy of God over his creation and in which we assume our own part of humanity and of the world as given by God and susceptible to change, social and historical.

In a way, the welcoming or non-welcoming of strangers measures our own understanding of the gospel and our trust or distrust of God. Numbers of Christians may decrease, numbers of immigrants may increase, and several faith communities outside Christianity may have a central role in our country: maybe this is God's plan, maybe that was already the plan unfolded on the day of Pentecost, when peoples of different nations and languages could understand the importance of the same words of resurrection, life and community-building. The Church was being shaped in a diversified and globalized manner quite different from religious sectarianism and over-emphasized nationalisms.

Political bodies

The media, once again, portrays on the one hand a Church that is dormant, irrelevant and outdated, while on the other it cries out in disbelief when church leaders express publicly the rights of faith communities to express their opinions and outline their choices within a democratic debate on legislation or constitutional issues. During 2007, for example, Cardinal O'Brien of Scotland spoke very strongly against abortion and criticized parliamentarians who, while being Catholics, did not do enough to challenge the current laws on abortion and the lawfulness of the act of abortion itself.

I was at that time contacted by the media office of the Scottish Parliament to seek my opinion about Cardinal O'Brien's behaviour. It is not a secret that I am a Roman Catholic, a practising one, and a friend of Cardinal O'Brien. Thus, my sense of the matter was that Cardinal O'Brien was correct to outline publicly the practices and beliefs of the Roman Catholic community, and to request further thinking on these matters from those who were part of the faith community he leads. The difficult part of this discussion was that the journalist put it to me that if a member of the Scottish Parliament was to represent his constituency he could not put his personal opinions above those of his constituents. My response was that while understanding that predicament, it was up to voters to re-elect or not re-elect their representatives. Within my own public life I have not found rejection from others because at times I have expressed my own sense of belonging to a particular faith community and tried within my human frailty and sinfulness to follow those tenets of faith.

There is some confusion about the relation between religion and politics, between the Churches and government. That confusion probably arises from a false dichotomy between the spiritual and the worldly part of life. In the UK, for example, the monarch remains the head of state and the head of the Church. Even when Scottish voters would immediately reply that the powers of government are devolved and therefore the Queen is just a symbolic figure, the fact is that Church and state remain connected in all public life. Constitutional changes are possible and sometimes constitutional affairs do not reflect the contemporary sense of the citizens; however, one cannot comment on the unknown future but only on the present. It is in this contemporary world that faith communities as the Body of Christ and individual Christians as members of that Body have the possibility, and I would argue the obligation, to participate in political life. After all, voters have the right to elect their representatives and should strive to do so in conscience by assessing political manifestos in the light of the gospel. No political party is directly connected with the values of the gospel, but some policies are closer to the attitudes of Jesus and the Kingdom of God than others.

It is clear that the Gospels portray Jesus as a person who moved with sinners and who had a preference for the poor and the marginalized and those who suffer – the sick, the possessed and those rejected by society. His ministry was not a spiritual-istic one, but his preaching was based on a changing attitude towards those preferred by his Father, and those who would enter the Kingdom first. He criticized those who were attached to their wealth and had forgotten the poor, and he made love of God and neighbour his political manifesto. He made de-mands on those who followed him, and he taught his disciples to pray while staying long hours in prayer himself, trying to comply with the will of his Father.

It is in relation to that model of life that Christians in their bodies and as political bodies need to operate. It is within those long periods of prayer and the contemplation of God as divine operator and Creator that Christians must find, as Jesus did, the will of the Father. The Gospels do not portray a sweet per-son who did not take part in society, nor do they portray an angry Jesus who stormed a place for ritual and prayer because the vendors and the merchants had taken it over. For those who cite the passage in Mark's Gospel where Jesus responds to the question of taxation – 'give to Caesar what is Caesar's and to God what is God's' – as a suggestion of his separation of the religious and the political, I provide a different understanding of the actual Gospel passage.

In the passage related to the tribute to Caesar (Mark 12.13–17), the Pharisees and the Herodians came to Jesus, and after asserting that he was an honest man not afraid of anyone, they asked him: 'Is it permissible to pay taxes to Caesar or not? Should we pay, yes or no?' Taking a coin, Jesus responded: 'Give back to Caesar what belongs to Caesar – and to God what belongs to God.'[8] I have written a longer commentary on this passage elsewhere,[9] but here it is sufficient to say that it is a passage that becomes key to understanding the relation between centre and periphery within Mark's Gospel, because it relates to a confrontation between religion and politics in which the consequences of Jesus' answer would either legitimize the oppressors or antagonize them by challenging the payment of taxes to the Roman governor.[10] Those who have separated the social realities of religion and politics have used this passage, or rather a misinterpretation of it. The dialectic of the question and of the answer points to a response by Jesus that takes the answer beyond the two given possibilities, that does not deny the centrality of religion and politics but points those reading Mark's Gospel to other values, other attitudes and other lives that have nothing to do with the centrality of government or religious organization, but with the Kingdom of God, that Kingdom already preached to the sinners and the marginalized that is not at the centre but within the periphery of the Jewish religion and of the Roman state. Indeed, for Carlos Bravo it is clear that 'the travesty the religious leaders make of God and his project is the principal obstacle to the people's hope'.[11]

Social memories, as outlined in the 'tribute', are fragments of social existence that continue recreating human expression and that in the case of areas such as religion and politics show an inconsistency that speaks of cultural and contextual constraints and contradictions. Even if Jesus disagreed with such taxation, he was forced to pay it and therefore his divine plans and messianic statements were dependent on political events that shaped not only his mission but the challenges of his opponents and the understanding of his hearers. On the one hand, studies of oral history suggest that people are capable of passing on stories and important memories; on the other, those memories are contextually recreated within a setting that cannot be the original one.

It is within such reframing of context that the 'tribute' appears contradictory, and Jesus is perceived as a clever respondent to his social challengers. His contextual setting is clear – a man who was a Jew and who believed in a God who was above emperors and kings, who had made a covenant with a particular people and who had established law and order as well as an institutional framework to that covenant through royal dynasties, divine laws and sacred spaces. Any of those Jewish perceptions could not be compromised; however, as happened with Josephus, either the colonial subject cooperated with the colonial power or was in trouble. Jesus' appeal within the 'tribute' is that he is able to live within two contested powers by suggesting that there are other social realities within a Kingdom that is not of this world, and in which neither Rome nor Jerusalem would be the leaders, but his Father.

The attitudes requested and spoken about by Jesus are life-changing parameters of acceptance of a peripheral world that is centred upon the poor and the marginalized and not upon the values of the market, celebrities or beauty pageants.

Bodily conditions

The media and the market aim at convincing everybody that cleaner, more cared for, more perfumed and more beautiful bodies are central to self and human existence. Anybody who has experienced peer pressure, particularly during their younger years in life, has experienced the power of the media and of the market. Advertising agencies play on the possibility that if we have one particular product we will feel better, look better and be better accepted by others. A point of clarification is in order here: I am not against aesthetic beauty and human beauty; on the contrary, I am the first to appreciate a crisp clean shirt and orderly hair. However, the question of what we need and what we don't need to be human has been dramatically confused by advertising campaigns, so that the assumption in our subconscious has become an equation between having the latest product and feeling human. The bodily conditions of selfhood and personhood, and therefore of humanness, within Christianity are slightly different.

We come from God and return to him; we are creatures with talents and beauty that have been given to us. And while we are supposed to be good stewards of our gifts, we must recognize at the end of the day the beauty of God in humanness, in nature, in sentient beings, in the cosmos and all creation. The body of God, currently understood as the planet itself, remains varied and beautiful to the human eye, and the whole of creation remains a song to God's creation. We are stewards not owners, and we are human beings not gods.

As a result, the human bodily condition creates the possibility of becoming more human while becoming more loving, more merciful and more Christian – all attributes and products of contemplation. It is the act of returning several times a day, not only on a Sunday, to a concrete engagement with God, with a personal being, with his Word and with his actions in the world. The encounter between a contemplative and his God is not solely an expression of the soul, but requires the submission of the body, the submission of time and space to the one who provides the full humanness of the encounter and the full loving activity in him. The surrendering of the human being in front of his creator is not strange to Muslims, and the emptying of oneself is not strange to Buddhists and Hindus. Thus, the act of setting aside time and space in order to spend time with one's creator unites us with people of other faiths and other persuasions because they bow to the centre of everything in the same way we do, by a body posture, a prayer, a creed, a moment in time, and with the sense of learning from the source of life and love himself.

Thomas Merton has expressed his own experience of contemplation and bodily submission in the following words:

> The unitive knowledge of God in love is not a knowledge of an object by a subject, but a far different and transcendent kind of knowledge in which the created 'self' which we are seems to disappear in God and to know him alone. In passive purification then the self undergoes a kind of emptying and an apparent destruction, until, reduced to emptiness, it no longer knows itself apart from God.[12]

Thus, Merton remarks that during prayer, meditation and contemplation it is not only the soul that turns to God but the whole body, because in order to communicate with their creator human beings do not pray with the mind as if acquiring information, but use their whole body, mind, soul and senses in order to feel united with their source of knowledge about the world. It is the body as a contemplative instrument that is able to bring the whole person with all his or her social contexts to a moment in which, by emptying oneself of other concerns, one can measure and experience the centrality of God and God's plan in all religious and political actions.

It is through personal and communal moments of prayer, contemplation and worship that human beings find their true humanness, and find God as central to their lives, their time and their spaces. For some traditions within the Church, that moment of central encounter takes place within the Eucharist celebrated in community, which is the subject of the following chapter.

8

The Eucharist and politics

At the conclusion of the 1986 film *The Mission* there is a poignant moment in which the Jesuits need to take a quick decision on account of the advancing Portuguese army. The Portuguese have decided on the closure of Jesuit missions in South America, and secured ownership of the indigenous peoples who had found refuge, education and a liberating Christianity under the protection of the Jesuits. A few Jesuits have organized an armed resistance against the incoming armies but lost against a large and well-equipped army. It is towards the end of the film, and when fires have already started in the mission buildings, that a lone Jesuit blesses the indigenous people with the Blessed Sacrament and advances towards the Portuguese. Will they murder this fully robed priest holding the Blessed Sacrament? Only briefly deterred, the Portuguese commander urges his fusiliers to shoot the priest, and he collapses to the ground. The contemplative moment lost, another Jesuit, a former mercenary and slave master, leads an armed rebellion. It too fails, but shows the two possible responses in the face of real life, a life informed by issues of religion and politics.

The Mission is an interpretation of a moment in history in which the Jesuits are forbidden to operate within the colonial empires because they have gone too far, defending the poor and marginalized by giving them education and human dignity. The Jesuits threatened the political establishment because they challenged the possibility of a total division between a divine and a human order. For the Jesuits of the *reducciones* (the settlements designed to Europeanize the indigenous population), the values of the Kingdom of God were to be implemented and realized within the legislation and social morality of human kingdoms that were to resemble the divine kingdom and the plans of the Divine King, an inspiration for activism that informed the political choices of contemporary Jesuits such as Daniel Berrigan.[1] The Eucharist was used as a symbolic reminder of the values of the Kingdom of God and as a symbolic political weapon in order to defend the poor.

This chapter extends that symbolic analysis so as to suggest that the Eucharist remains a symbolic bridge between the human and the divine, between religion and politics in contemporary society.[2] Communities that celebrate the Eucharist learn the values of communion and of justice and peace that belong to the feast of the Kingdom of God, by performing the memorial actions of Jesus – breaking bread and sharing wine – and reinforcing symbolic and social action as an extension of the 'Do this in memory of me'. After learning together, members of those communities go into the human world challenging those attitudes and values that contradict the values of the Kingdom of God; that is, the values of a common humanity blessed by God, in which all are sons and daughters of God with a human dignity that is given by God and that cannot be ignored by particular governments or particular social groups associated with political exclusion and discrimination. The Eucharist becomes a celebration of the Kingdom of God but also a political symbol within human society. Where there are Eucharistic communities, God's presence is assured within society and members of those communities exercise their right of political influence by bringing to political decisions their own sense of the values and the social morality of the Kingdom of God (see also the next chapter, on contemplation and voting).

The politics of the Eucharist

In his insightful book *Torture and Eucharist*, William Cavanaugh explores the political and sacramental realities of torture in Chile when Augusto Pinochet was in power (1973–90). His sharp theological analysis relates the rites and rituals of the Eucharist as a sacrament to the rites and rituals of torture as a state symbol that builds new citizens obedient and docile through a 'kind of perverted liturgy'.[3] Within that analysis, Cavanaugh is critical of the possible relation between the realms of liturgy and politics as 'to enter the political is to leave the liturgical'. Further, Cavanaugh understands the liturgical as creating community and motivating people to create a better world with a clear division between the religious and the political: 'Attempts to relate liturgy and politics, or some similar combination, are often admirable but fail to overcome the kind of dichotomies they seek to bridge.'[4] His emphasis is on incorporation of individual bodies into a larger body, the Body of Christ, that seems already shaped into form physically and metaphysically. Cavanaugh's sharp historical, social and theological analysis could have reached the opposite conclusions, but he chose to affirm a dichotomy of contemplation and life that, in my analysis of the same period in history, I have seen as a clear example of the interwoven social relations and political action that comes out of the powerful Eucharistic symbolism.[5]

The weakness of such an analysis is the same weakness that has made possible the mental processes whereby ordinary people, and indeed lay Christians, have come to accept a given division between religion and politics. Within that false division, the Body of Christ has been identified either with the Word of God in the reformed traditions, or with the Eucharist in the widely theologically understood Catholic world. Following Cavanaugh's argument, those involved in the political world have decided to find symbols of God's presence outside the Body of Christ, rather than within. By suggesting that symbols of the divine and Eucharistic symbols of the feast of the Kingdom of Heaven could be found within the social and political spheres, they have left behind the liturgical richness and the sole consolation of the truth found in 'the breaking of bread'.

Cavanaugh understands the contemplative dimension of suffering within politics, and his own larger discussion of the role of the Christian community within contemporary society has been an extension of the complex theological discussions by Jewish theologians on the presence or absence of God within the concentration camps where the European Holocaust of the twentieth century took place.[6] Within a divided religion and politics, sacred and profane, or private and public worlds, God is not present – he is absent from the messy realms of social reality and gives way to the evil doers who challenge the power of grace and the involvement of an incarnated God. I disagree with that interpretation: the God of the poor remains within the filth and the social sin of society, and in a mysterious way decides not to intervene in order to destroy the evil doers.[7] The God of the poor decides to immerse himself in a body, he is born of a woman, he suffers thirst and pain, he is killed and finally he is raised by his Father. Within that incarnational principle of divine providence, any theology of the body recognizes that without a body there is no salvation, be it social, human or divine (see also the previous chapter).[8]

If Cavanaugh explores the possibility of divisions between the liturgical and the political, I would prefer to stress their socio-religious continuity. They remain separate realms of action and thought, with different symbols and symbolic actions, but they remain interwoven in a circle of hermeneutics, a circle of interpretive suspicion that creates a better context for the realms of religion and of politics. My proposed framework suggests that a binary opposition between Mother Teresa's model of contemplation and Daniel Berrigan's model of politics does not need to exist within a cyclical model of contemplation and politics. I rely here on the methodologies proposed by liberation theology, where the Eucharist is the centre of reflection and action for different members of the community: for those who have felt compelled to go from Eucharist to politics and those who have come to the Eucharist through a deep involvement in politics and the social organization of society. In fact, there are two ways of understanding the relation between religion and politics: from faith to politics or from politics to faith.

Too much stress has been put on the separation of those two ways rather than on their continuity; however, there is only one way of stressing the symbolism of community, and that is by reasserting the importance of the Trinitarian symbolism of Father, Son and Holy Spirit in communion, where all the actions of the Eucharistic memorial require the community action of the three persons of the Trinity, while in response the community learns new ways of communion with the Triune God and with the world. Eucharistic communities become political communities because they go forth into the world to transform it and to make it more and more into the image of God's communion. Without the Eucharistic sense of community, individuals toil alone in a personal commitment to grace, but without the strength of the communal God that comes to a communal world where the aim is to welcome *all* and to celebrate a fellowship with sinners and saints together with the Triune God. In the words of Míguez Bonino:

> Common celebration, reflection, and action are the cradle of a new personal identity. The nonperson claims and is given 'the word', the right to speak and be heard. He or she becomes a subject of decisions. God announces the Word in this person's reading and responding to the gospel. The Holy Spirit builds the ekklesia as such persons come and celebrate together. Thus, one's personal identity is not created over against 'the others' but together with them. And social identity is not achieved by suppressing the individual (as in the mass) but by projecting and acting together in freedom.[9]

I stress here the possibility and the actuality of a Eucharistic celebration that brings together not only cultural elements meaningful to the congregation that celebrates the Eucharist, but also their daily concerns, both at the individual level and at the larger social and political level. Leonardo Boff, stressing the importance of the Eucharist within the Brazilian Small Christian Communities, outlines the fact that their joyful cele-

bration and encounters with other communities are meaningful because they bring the context and the politics of place and
social identity to the actual liturgical celebration. Boff describes
a day of meetings between different Christian communities
and emphasizes in the following manner the impact they had
on him:

> The most profound experiences of the day in Itaici were with-
> out a doubt the celebrations in the morning, and especially
> the Eucharist in the evening. They were encounters of a deep,
> joyful faith, where, in the Paschal Mystery, everything was
> celebrated that had happened during the day.[10]

There is a 'raised consciousness' that comes out of the reading
of the Bible within those communities, rather than via infiltra-
tion from leftist agents. Thus, Boff comments:

> The Bible was written in communities of poor people, nearly
> always under the domination of foreign powers and yearning
> for integral liberation. At Itaici one would hear, 'God is polit-
> ical, but he's fair – look at Exodus 3.7': 'I have witnessed the
> affliction of my people in Egypt, and I have heard their cry of
> complaint against their slave drivers . . . Therefore I have come
> to rescue them . . .'. (Exodus 3.7–8)[11]

The sign of the Kingdom

There are several ways of celebrating the Eucharist following
Christ's command at the last supper and the Pauline instructions to build the body of Christ. However, in all cases the centrality of sharing bread and wine emerges as an occasion for
Christian fellowship and for the integration of community
members into a liturgical and sacramental moment of grace. In
Roman Catholicism, the Eucharist remains a central moment
that makes both the Church and the community, and unlike
other Christian groups, Catholics are encouraged to celebrate
the Eucharist daily with their priests. The 1972 Catholic Rites
settled the use of the vernacular languages for the celebration
of the Eucharist and integrated signs and symbols within the

liturgy by which lay people were encouraged to participate more actively through readings, prayers, offerings, songs and, in the case of Africa, dances.

The Eucharist as communion and as rite of passage binds Christians with one another, with God and with the Church, making them a distinctive group with a particular social identity, but a varied group in their political views and actions within both the nation/state and the social realms of party politics. It is clear that the Kingdom of God is a larger mystical reality than a particular Christian community and a particular church; however, its central symbol of unity is the Eucharist, where the 'fellowship with sinners' is actualized once and again, and where Christ comes once and again to embrace, to redeem and to save. That moment of salvation cannot be solely a personal one, but reflects a community experience of Christ eating and drinking with his disciples before his supreme sacrifice on the cross and his subsequent resurrection. Indeed, the contemporary understanding of the communal celebration of the Eucharist 'is its community character. It brings Christians together in the name of Jesus and involves the active participation of God's people in the Eucharist.'[12]

The political challenges of contemplation

The act of contemplation has been for centuries a Christian practice. At the highest levels, Christian mystics such as St Teresa of Avila or St John of the Cross have experienced the joys and pains of coming face to face with God. They have striven for an intimate encounter, and in doing so have ascended the Holy Mountain with the physical and emotional pain of trying to love and trying to understand the demands of the beloved. At another level, religious communities of men and women have come together to contemplate the divine, helped by the reciting of the daily prayers of the Church and the daily celebration of the Eucharist. Among them the most austere, such as the Carthusians, have embraced a communal living in which each person strives in silence to reach a higher level of contemplation of the divine, following the desert fathers, who chose solitude and silence in order to encounter God. A participant in the television series *The Monastery* experienced the life of the Carthusians for a month, and reflecting on his experience said:

> To be truly silent, to avoid all needless preoccupation with the past and the future, to just be in the here and now, is to be present to God, to encounter God in the silent emptiness that is the heart of our being; where, emptied of ourselves, we can share in His being. Even people who do not believe in God would surely agree that there is something very interesting about the fact that most of the time we are simply not present, either to ourselves or each other, never mind God.[13]

The daily contemplation of God by Christians arises out of prayer, prayer that is not necessarily different from ordinary parish prayer, but which searches for God rather than for the fulfilment of routines or ritualized forms of self-affirmation. It is a courageous form of prayer because it empties itself of any other distractions and asks God face to face: 'Who are you?' and 'What do you want of me?' The contemplative road to such a moment of direct contemplative awareness is not difficult; however, it takes a particular will to reach a direct communication with a God of surprises, a God of silence or a God who demands responses that are sometimes dangerous and not necessarily of personal reaffirmation. It is the road taken by the men and women described in the previous chapters: their road of prayer and silent contemplation led them to dangerous actions that were not always necessarily legal (Sheila Cassidy and Daniel Berrigan SJ) or quiet (Archbishop Tutu), or that were misunderstood by the Church (Ernesto Cardenal), by their religious superiors (Thomas Merton) or by political powers (Mother Teresa). They became examples of prayer, contemplation and politics because they followed a difficult path through a constant dialogue with a God who was asking from them responses that they had never thought they wanted to give in the first place. The same challenge is faced by thousands of Christians today, by those who take seriously the road to a direct communication with God, a God who calls humans as instruments of divine intervention within the Church and within the political realms of society.

The political challenges of the Eucharist

If the Eucharist is the highest possible prayer of thanksgiving and intercession, then it is also the favourite place for that encounter between a Christian community and God. It is in that messianic feast that God speaks through the Word of God, in which God nourishes his people through bread and wine and in which those present are sent forth in peace, not to rest but to continue the work of the Kingdom. In many places in Latin America and Africa, the communal celebration of the Eucharist has become a moment in which the signs and symbols of the Christian liturgies have represented a public challenge to unjust political social orders.

That was the case in South Africa, where the homilies and liturgies presided over by Archbishop Tutu attacked the unjust apartheid regime by speaking of a Kingdom where all had a place and where all were equal in the eyes of God. It is difficult to say that such a Christian proclamation of justice and peace embedded in the Kingdom of God was not a political act as well as a prophetic Christian witness. After all, the aim of such prophetic proclamation was to change an unjust social system and make it into a socially and morally acceptable egalitarian one. In South Africa, the language of Christian forgiveness was used even by the Commission of Truth and Reconciliation, heavily influenced by the personality of Archbishop Tutu and his Christian ideas of politics within South African society.

There is no doubt that in the lives of all those great Christian personalities who give gospel witness in society, a great deal of prayer is involved, solitary and courageous encounter with a God who requests more from them than they think they can give. The Chilean cardinal, Raúl Silva Henríquez, for example, was perceived as the only public figure who mobilized a local church in order to challenge Pinochet's abuses of human rights, and he defended and saved the lives of many of the regime's political opponents and those it persecuted. His prayer started very early in the morning, followed by the celebration of the Eucharist in his private chapel. Only after those ritual actions had been performed was he able to start his day, usually a very public day of engagements and meetings.[14] However, when things got rough, and once he had been challenged by other Chilean bishops on his actions of constant opposition to the regime, he brought his friend Reinaldo Sapag to his chapel and, standing in front of the Blessed Sacrament, asked God why he was doing this to him. He reminded God in a loud voice that God had called him and that he had tried to serve; thus, he needed a bit more reassurance and support if he was to survive the difficult times ahead![15]

Contemporary challenges

It is my suggestion that prayer and contemplation lead to a public commitment, to a social responsibility and to political action. If the contemplative religious communities pray and offer sacrifices for the sanctification of the rest of the universal Church, individual Christians worshipping in community find their way of action out of their own commitment to constant prayer and to the contemplation of the divine. The celebration of the Eucharist becomes the place where a taste of the Kingdom of God is acquired and where the 'now' and the 'not yet' of the Kingdom's life is realized.

The challenge for every Christian and for every community is to realize that there is a link between contemplation as the act of personal prayer and politics as Christian action in the world. That world is not an abstract world but the world around us, where we live, where our children are educated, where we pay taxes, where policies regarding our environment and our future existence within society are proposed, discussed and implemented. Here I can comprehend no division between religion and politics. Leaders of churches and politicians have a role to play in the devising of democratic policies that have been discussed and sometimes challenged by both the values of the gospel and the values of the Kingdom of God that arise out of personal contemplation and the communal celebration of the Eucharist. In Britain in particular, where Anglican bishops are part of the House of Lords and where the Queen is the head of the Church of England, it is very difficult to justify why Christians should not see connections between religion and politics, between following a religious rule and a Christian way of life together with their own active participation in the decisions that inform the government of the *polis* – of society in general.

It is through the Eucharist that Christians discover contemporary challenges to social problems of poverty, hunger, disease or Christian challenges to abortion or euthanasia, nuclear weapons or environmental disasters, because it is at the Eucharist that the Word of God speaks of a utopian world in which there will be no more hunger or disease and where God will be one with all. If in the past the coming of that utopian Kingdom was a sign of realities to come in the future, there has been a general understanding that through the incarnation of the Son of God he was made flesh and therefore became one of us in all things but sin. Thus, our task and our response to the Word and to the Word made flesh in the Eucharist is to follow and imitate the Christ of the Gospels: he mingled with sinners and prostitutes, he ate and drank with his disciples and he was even prepared to use violence at the sight of sellers within the Temple in Jerusalem. The Son of God was the first to challenge the powers of the state and the powers of the Temple by suggesting that they were not opposed, but that his messianic banquet and the Kingdom of God, while being higher realities to come, were yet already among us in some imperfect form.

In the words of the Archbishop of Cali, Colombia, in 2005, during the 11th Ordinary General Assembly of the Synod of Bishops in Rome:

> The Eucharist is the answer to the negative signs of contemporary culture. In the first place in contrast with the culture

or anti-culture of death which traffics in arms, builds massive systems of destruction, legitimizes abortion and authorizes research using human embryos, Jesus defines himself and gives himself to us as 'Bread of Life'. Secondly, our culture is marked with hatred and terrorism: 11 September, 11 March, the London Underground . . . the Eucharist is the permanent possibility of reconciliation with God and our brothers and sisters, and the invitation to reconcile ourselves with one another before offering worship to the Lord . . .[16]

In practice, how do we do this? How do we deepen our understanding of the need to depart from a Eucharistic celebration devoid of action? I would suggest that a moment of daily prayer is the essence of that fruitful connection between worship and action, between the practice of religion and the practice of politics – both necessary daily practices. That moment of prayer needs to be at the centre of busy lives; thus, it needs to be inbuilt in our electronic organizers, diaries, kitchen reminders and computer updates. For a number of Christians, for example, checking emails is a daily practice that enables them to keep in touch with friends and relatives or to respond to ever-increasing demands related to work or keeping up to date with new information. We check our emails regularly and feel in touch with others; we know what our friends are going through and what they wish at that moment of their lives. Prayer has the same movement of connectivity with God, in that every day we check our own journey against his wishes, designs and feelings. If in an email we ask 'How are you?' we also ask God every day for his feelings, designs and plans while sharing our journey with him and with others.

Daily prayer becomes contemplation when our own desires and preoccupations start taking a secondary place and we focus more and more on what God wants of us and of his world. Thus, despite our own selfish desires for happiness and comfort, we find ourselves striving for what God wants for his world and, as in the case of Daniel Berrigan, we start risking our own comfort in order to help recreate God's world, and we continue looking after others instead of ourselves. Praying the psalms is particularly meaningful because most of them incorporate metaphors and images of nature, of the world and of human feelings that we have all experienced at one point or another. If the world needs more Christian activists, they will only come to the fore because more Christian contemplatives are deeply rooted in meaningful moments of worship and Eucharistic moments of prophecy, moments in which we challenge the established order of consumption and greed by allowing a touch of a utopian world to come through the Eucharist.

In the following chapter I examine the political role of Christians via the exercise of their right (and their obligation) to vote, and how their participation in political parties has been a sign of lay Christian involvement in the building of the Kingdom of God here and now.

9

Lay contemplatives and voters: a daily pilgrimage

In the previous chapters I have explored the relation between contemplative bodies and their political actions within particular periods for contemplation and times for the celebration of the Eucharist. Thus, I have argued that lay contemplatives following in the tradition of the Church's contemplative action in the world become political bodies who, in their act of voting, become part of a larger community identified as the Body of Christ in contemporary society. In this final chapter I want to explore how to organize one's core values of contemplation and politics within everyday life, since only a few have had access either to a spiritual director or a communal structure for reciting the daily office or morning and evening prayers. I rely here on my own practice of contemplation over 25 years as a pragmatic approach to contemplation and politics rather than as a high theology of the religious life or of contemplative praise of the divine beauty of God. I hope that after reading several chapters in which I have outlined narratives of pastoral theology, the reader might take a moment to reassess the daily practices, priorities and contemplative periods within his or her own contemporary way of life within a larger pilgrimage from God and towards God that has a past, a present and a future.

A daily contemplative pilgrimage

In his insightful book on monastic prayer, *Finding Sanctuary*, the Benedictine Abbot Christopher Jamison spoke of the need for sanctuary, for a place within the home or within the lunch-time break at work where one can find 'sanctuary' and connect with God. Further, he recognized that 'there are two classic moments for enjoying silence: the early morning and night time', so that 'you can build a time of silence into your morning or night routine. A real help here is to have a physical sanctuary area somewhere in your living space.'[1]

One would hope that the television series *The Monastery*, in which Abbot Jamison was a central player, awakened many Christians to the possibility of encountering God more closely within their daily lives. In my opinion, what is needed, apart from good intentions, is a contemplative health-check that first, over a period of 24 hours, analyses the actual priorities and movements of a person's daily activities. Again, this varies according to age and state in life, so that for example those who are older arguably have more freedom to dispose their activities, while young parents must have as a central priority the welfare and growth of their children.

In the monastic tradition, as in all religious communities and the life of priests and vicars, the praying of the Divine Office, a book containing hymns, psalms, intercessory prayers and special offices for important days within the liturgical calendar, marks the hours of the day. The Second Vatican Council encouraged Christians to pray the Divine Office and also to mark the hours of the day with morning, evening and night prayer, and the first spiritual health-check above relates to the actual time that we spend in prayer daily. If this looks like overdoing it, one should remember that Muslims have the obligation to pray five times a day, and their daily routine is ordered towards that aim. If Christian practice and prayer were only to relate to the obligation to worship on a Sunday, there would never be a connection between Christian life and social life, knowing that in general most people have to spend more time at work than with their families or children, or in prayer. Thus, the balance between action and contemplation does not depend only on the will of the individual but on the possibility of reflecting on the centrality of God in our lives and the steps that can reasonably be taken to respect and order that centrality.

Thus, for Thomas Merton, commenting on the writings of St Bernard: 'if the charity of the apostle is superior to that of the contemplative, there is only one reason: it is a *development* of contemplative charity, a *fruit* of contemplation.'[2]

The main times to spend a moment in the presence of God are the morning and the evening. However, it has to become a daily habit of praying a psalm, chatting to God about things or witnessing God's beauty in creation with thanksgiving. Once the habit is there, moments of tiredness, stress and even anger will all be related to those moments of contemplation and prayer. Thus, routines are inevitable. We say that we don't like routines but we all have them – football on Saturdays for some, weekend walks for others. There are moments and activities in each person's life that others are encouraged to respect. Even going to church on a Sunday becomes a given for others, such as friends or family, who might refrain from issuing an invitation for a Sunday-morning event because they know a particular family goes to church then.

Once patterns of morning and evening prayer become as natural as having a cup of tea, there is the possibility of spending a period of communication and intimacy with God at lunch-time. That could be done at work: mentally, by taking a moment away from everything; physically, by going for a short walk to a park or a nearby church. Once again, the actual location or length of the intimate moment is less important than the habit of relying on that moment as central to the person's life. For all contemplation – and action – relies on the free will of a Christian who decides once and for all that God is central to his or her life, thus making every action and every moment relate to that reality. Then we start our pilgrimage, in which we are aware that we are preparing to return to our Father, and the Father of all, or to our Mother, symbolically expressed through the complexity, diversity and universality of the Church as a tapestry of faith communities, languages and customs all over the world.

Patterns of sleep dictate the possibility of a night conversation with God; a thought and a prayer before collapsing totally after a day's parenthood or work are as good as a period of listening to the silence of the evening or the chatting of happy souls leaving the pub in the early hours. Silence does not denote the absence of sound but the opening of one's soul to the all-embracing face of God, who protects and cares for the stranger, the poor and the lonely. In moments of fear and uncertainty, the habit of intimate conversation or silence makes all the difference because the centrality of God becomes the safety of the known within ever-changing personal situations.

I remember buying a copy of *Finding Sanctuary* at a book-shop in Princes Street, Edinburgh, and having to wait at Hunter Square for the arrival of a loved one. As I started reading the book, a total stranger sat beside me on the same bench and asked me if I had enjoyed the day. In that moment was Christ the stranger asking me the question? Maybe so, but there is no doubt that the fact of taking a moment away from everything to read and be close to God made that encounter possible. The spiritual health-check that I propose aims at the same question: do we have moments in which God can sit with us for a short while? It is through those moments that we find deeper happiness and feel wholesome and human. Finally, we are on our pilgrimage and we know where we are going; there is a purpose in our lives, and that is the company of God and the love of God, through us, for our neighbour and for the stranger within every community, every street and every nation of this world.

The politics of the stranger

It is from this experience of daily contemplation that our political and social life arises. Once the political manifesto or the white paper has been published, we return to a conversation with God; we return to the sacred texts and to the quietness of our hearts, and we ponder about the following action: voting not for the sake of a party, not for the sake of power or prestige, but in order to enhance God's care for the poor, the marginalized and the stranger. It is the act of voting that becomes a fruit of contemplation and an important moment in which we, as God's instruments, try to take a small step, an ordinary step, in order to build up a society in which God can live and in which God can protect the vulnerable of society.

How do we know if political views are actually consistent with the gospel? This is both clear and essentially complex. If we assume and accept that the Gospels portray a Jesus who is calling disciples to exercise a continuous and daily encounter with sinners and with strangers, there is no doubt that some of the compromised values of Christianity within contemporary life come out. Two passages are important: the first is the calling of Jesus in the synagogue in which, reading the scroll of the prophet Isaiah, he feels the call to bring good news to the poor; the second is the text of the beatitudes – blessed are those who are poor or have the spirit of poverty but alas for the rich, they have already received their reward.

Contemplation as a daily activity remains connected with a public daily proclamation of the values of the gospel through a lifestyle that connects with those gospel values. Simplicity and self-sacrifice for others do not seem to be the highest values in contemporary society, but they are values intrinsic to Jesus' tableship with sinners and the calling of his disciples. The early Church experienced those values as Christians were persecuted. They shared what they had and they welcomed slaves and the poor of the Roman Empire. Indeed, the strength of the gospel was that those despised by Roman society were welcomed to the Kingdom of the Father as well as the learned and the powerful citizens of Rome, as in the case of the apostle Paul after his conversion to 'the Way' on the road to Damascus.

Here, let me point out a couple of obstacles that I see in the contemporary practice of Christianity. First, the changes in contemporary society, while of concern to the churches, are not ultimately responsible for the decline in Christian practice. It is the possibility that for a larger number of people Christianity is not central to their lives that is of concern, and that sociological fact can only be amended by a movement towards people, towards the stranger and towards the marginalized, rather than by hundreds of calls to find Jesus as Saviour in a personal manner. Indeed, the born-again Christian who gives testimony of Christ in his life, and the Evangelical who preaches a Christianity of no drinking, no dancing and no sociability, do not portray the Christ of the Gospels, who takes part in weddings, rejoices over the penitent sinner and finds friendship and intimacy with his friends at the house of Lazarus, Martha and Mary. Second, if the practice of Christianity becomes disassociated from the realities of human life then it does not follow the understanding of the universal Church and thus of the great councils of the Church that declared that Jesus of Nazareth and the Christ of faith were one person and that Christ was 'true God and true man'. If Christianity is in decline in Europe it is because people of their own free will have decided to search for answers to life somewhere else. It is only through a deep contemplative life, and through action within our daily life and community life, that we will bring the message of Christ to others. However, it is only God who can provide the graces for a person to believe and to follow. We are only instruments and stewards of God's creation. In welcoming the stranger, the immigrant, the unloved, the prisoner and the frail and sick, we welcome Christ. It is in those actions that the revival of any church community lies.

Contemplation and ecological issues

One of the major issues that seems to engage all nations and all people nowadays is that of global warming. Maybe a discussion of this issue will highlight the role of contemplative Christians in the contemporary world. Regardless of those who deny the connection between gas emissions and global warming related to climate change, theologians such as the Brazilian Leonardo Boff have previously stressed ecological issues in relation to a human stewardship – not an ownership – of the planet. Thus, Boff pays attention to detailed ecological issues related to Amazonia in the light of the biblical narratives of creation, and of human beings as co-creators with the Creator but at the end solely creatures vis-à-vis the Creator. Boff writes:

> Beginning a new covenant with the Earth absolutely requires a reclaiming of the dimension of the sacred. Without the sacred, affirming the dignity of Earth and the need to set limits on our desire to exploit its potentialities remains empty rhetoric. The sacred is a founding experience. It underlies the great experiences on which the cultures of the past and indeed the underlying identity of the human being have been built.[3]

It is human greed and human exploitation, overfishing, over-grazing and indiscriminate felling of the rain forests that have made us realize that the resources of the planet are limited, and have led to concerns about future generations and ourselves. These concerns have been discussed within different political agendas and some international proposals are coming through. However, the Christian responsibility for those who live under the umbrella of the G-8 nations is greater because lay contemplative voters can influence the policies passed by their democratically elected representatives. It is a Christian responsibility to preserve God's creation, and moments of contemplation help us to read the biblical narratives of creation in the book of Genesis and the beautiful canticles and songs of praise that the people of Israel composed, known as the Psalms, in order to praise God for the beauty of creation. Let us take an example from Psalm 148.7–9:

> Let earth praise Yahweh:
> Sea-monsters and all the deeps,
> Fire and hail, snow and mist,
> Gales that obey his decree,
> Mountains and hills,
> Orchards and forests,
> Wild animals and farm animals,
> Snakes and birds.

The exuberant moment of contemplation of God's creation brings in itself a joy and a humanness that makes us happier and stronger. Those who live in large urban centres long for a break in the countryside or on the beach, while those who live by the sea treasure the possibility of a daily contemplation of God's creation. I must confess that I live a few blocks away from the beach and from open expansive views of the ocean. It surprises me that every day the sea has a different colour and that every day the sound of the waves, the birds and the water connects with the God of creation through the different motions and moods of each particular day. The stormy sea on a cloudy day reminds me of the dangers of those at sea and the dangers and turmoil of our daily life. However, the challenge is not to remain absorbed by the beauty of creation but to dialogue with the Creator about his creation.

It is here that I return to the close link between those contemplative periods of the day, in my case by the sea, and the presence of the Creator who urges us in an intimate dialogue to take care of his creation and therefore to try to influence those who claim ownership of the sea, of fish and of every part of creation. Ultimately, in our Christian understanding, creation and the planet belong to God and not to the multinational corporations or to those who kill human beings and animals in order to gain property, profit and prestige.

A word of caution at this point: if the reader feels that this is too utopian or detached from reality, then I would suggest that a good spiritual health-check is needed. Faith communities believe in the primacy of God, and work within society in order to collaborate in shaping a society that follows the attitudes that Jesus preached and that have been recorded in the Gospels; that is, those attitudes associated with the Kingdom of God, with the Reign of God. However, faith communities do not believe in avoiding a daily engagement with policy-making, with decision-making and with laws that affect God's creation, because they have been entrusted with that creation, its conservation, respect and co-creation.

Contemplation and the poor

Jesus' ministry towards the poor and the marginalized summarizes the three qualities that keep a daily contemplation alive: self-awareness in the context of the world; intimacy with God; and questioning of the relation between the world and God.

I have said enough about the periods of contemplation and the relation between God, his world and our stewardship. I return now to issues of Christian and human self-awareness within contemplation and politics. Much stress has been laid on individuality and self-awareness within contemporary Europe. We are supposed to be individuals, and most of our teenage years and formative years in adulthood are full of social and personal explorations in which we attempt to respond to – not comply with – other peoples, other ideas, other ways of doing things and other diverse understandings of God, the world, society, politics and the meaning of life.

Many times over the past few years I have been asked: 'Who are the poor?' Most people tend to associate the poor with the materially poor only, and indeed we have them in every country. In the UK, they might be those who are on income support and don't see a way out, such as a single mother unable to look for work because she cannot afford care for her children. In the USA, they might be the ethnically segregated who long for home and can't find it, or the political immigrant traumatized by a serious experience of war or terror who has enough materially but can't find meaning in life. In the Third or Fourth Worlds (the latter in the sense of countries with no natural resources that might enable them to develop), where the majority of the planet's poor live, they might be the millions of people without security, without water, electricity or enough to eat. In general, the poor are those who, in their poverty, trust in God because they do not have any other supporter, and they have the same rights as everybody else because, as everybody else, they were created and are loved by God.

The principle of social and economic inequality is what makes some people poor and others accepted and beautiful. Those who have want more; those who have less are usually the subject of natural disasters, sickness, deprivation and further poverty. It is to those dispossessed – the majority of the world – that Jesus showed particular compassion, solidarity and attention. If Latin American theologians, for example, spoke about 'God's preferential option for the poor', it was because the Gospels show an itinerant Jesus who spends more time with the sick, the sinners, the poor and the possessed than with well-to-do people able to welcome him at their homes and maybe to pay him a stipend for occasional teaching, as he had a reputation of being a teacher.

It is in relation to the people to whom Jesus gave more time – the poor and the marginalized – that contemplation and intimacy with God ultimately direct themselves. For in speaking and listening to God and in exalting his divine beauty, we are sent into the world to share with Jesus the proclamation of good news. In contemplation we turn to the Word of the same God in order to focus on the instructions he gives his followers regarding the world, a world of God, created and inhabited by God. The followers of Christ have the potential to influence policies that affect the poor and the marginalized, but they also have a mandate to show solidarity with them, to embrace them and to care for them, because they represent the face of Christ.

Let me return to the man who sat beside me on a bench in Edinburgh while I was reading Abbot Jamison's *Finding Sanctuary*. He was from North America and wore a US flag, but there was something odd about him, signs of being uncared for, of being a man rejected by others; he had filthy nails and smelled. He told me how beautiful life was and how reading about spiritual things was good for the world. Once I saw that my loved ones had arrived I said goodbye and moved on. I still wonder if he was Christ on the streets of Edinburgh; I still wonder if that was a moment of contemplative reaffirmation in which messages from the divine had been exchanged. I can't be certain, but I can be certain that daily contemplation and intimate conversations with God bring a different sense to streets and cities, which no longer seem frightening but rather filled with God's sons and daughters. Edinburgh is particularly poignant because along Princes Street and the Royal Mile, one encounters people from all over the world, while there are many selling *The Big Issue* (the magazine sold by homeless people), many drunkards, prostitutes and unemployed youth. They represent the face of Christ and they walk our streets trying to show us the face of God.

In previous chapters I have outlined the courageous and inspiring commitment by outstanding Christians to the gospel through their contemplative and public life of service to others. The figures of Thomas Merton, Ernesto Cardenal, Daniel Berrigan SJ, Sheila Cassidy, Archbishop Tutu and Mother Teresa remind us that contemplation and politics, personal sanctification and service to others go together. I still don't know where the individualistic sense of Christianity comes from, where a personal God without connections is found by those who, having been 'saved', speak only of their joy and their salvation while there are millions – also sons and daughters of God, loved and cherished by him – living in the most despicable conditions.

Matthew 25.31–46 outlines the realities of the last judgement; that is, of the encounter between a human being and his creator at the end of a biological life. At a time when all sorts of details and proscriptions were important for the keepers of the Jewish Law, Jesus told his listeners very clearly that he had not come to abolish the Law but to fulfil it, and his teachings were as direct as those in this passage in Matthew: love of God implies love of neighbour as well. This is an important passage for an ongoing spiritual health-check, because in times of spiritual enthusiasm and sometimes self-centredness, it demonstrates the centrality of the good news in the relationship between God, ourselves and others, particularly the dispossessed, the poor and the marginalized of this world. The passage reads as follows:

> Then the King will say to those on his right hand, 'Come, you whom my Father has blessed, take for your heritage the kingdom prepared for you since the foundation of the world. For I was hungry and you gave me food; I was thirsty and you gave me drink; I was a stranger and you made me welcome; naked and you clothed me, sick and you visited me, in prison and you came to see me.'   (Matthew 25.34–36)

When the King is asked about the occasions on which those who did not recognize him could have seen him, he replies: 'I tell you solemnly, in so far as you did this to one of the least of these brothers of mine, you did it to me' (Matthew 25.40). This is the message for all lay contemplatives: the measure of your contemplation is the extension of God's actions through you towards the poor. Contemplation and solitude act then as motivators and possible catalysts of the human soul, a soul already turning to God and to one another that needs continuing encouragement and divine nourishment, not for the sake of the soul's content but for others' nourishment, life and journey from God and towards God. For it is those moments of solitude and contemplation that become central to the formation and nourishment of the Christian who normally lives in the world and acts within a world of faith and politics, a contradictory world that after all belongs to God and provides divine encouragement to all, Christians and non-Christians, believers, atheists or agnostics alike.

Contemplation, solitude and politics

It could be argued that the three processes of contemplation, solitude and politics share in common human and divine processes that signify much more than meets the human eye and the human experience in the first instance. For as I have argued in the previous chapters, the six contemplatives chosen for discussion here have gone through the three processes and have led by example, even when they didn't realize what example they were setting for others at the time of their actions.

It was probably Thomas Merton who systematized the relation between the three processes by seeking solitude at the
Abbey of Gethsemani, by experiencing the depths of contemplation over several years and by assuming that his status as
Christian writer and American celebrity should be used for the
purpose of highlighting the need to stop war by continuing
reflection on issues of religion and politics. With all that personal influence, what else was he to do in a country such as the
USA, where religion and politics remain constitutionally separated but humanly connected?

According to Merton's biographer, Michael Mott, several
questions dominated periods of Merton's life: What is the effect-
ive peaceful alternative to violence? How can we prevent social
injustice? What can we learn from other religious traditions?[4]
Merton craved solitude but had little privacy in a strict monastic community, based on medieval models and still, by the
1940s, without private cells. Within that experience, contemplation arising out of prayer had to be negotiated within a
whole group of people who surrounded Merton in the chapel,
as well as through the communal activities of the day. It was
only in the 1960s that Merton was allowed to have his own
hermitage within the land of the Abbey, a hermitage that acted
as an ecumenical and meeting place for many activities that the
Trappists wanted to carry out after the reforms to religious life
triggered by the Second Vatican Council.

It is this early period of Merton's life that is important for
the ordinary lay contemplative and voter. Within this period
Merton grew in a prayerful intimacy with God by a strict use of
his time, so that he recognized that when he had a maximum
two hours a day for reading and writing in the 1950s, he wrote
more than when he could organize his own activities in the
1960s. He never liked the word contemplation but didn't find
any better word to express those moments in which God and a
particular human being meet in total connection, without the
worries and anxieties of the world.

Towards the end of his life, Merton's politics were the politics of God, and he could not be constrained by a hermit's life

without engagement with the world. His dramatic accidental death followed a very dramatic life. It is here that one must connect the life of Christian celebrities with that of ordinary people. No life is ordinary because every life is precious to God. No life is ordinary because each human being grows into the same pattern of the Christ who searches for happiness and friendship with others; however, as in the case of Merton, Jesus also dies in a dramatic fashion on a cross. It is the untimely possibilities of all human beings that make the journey of contemplation and politics a very exciting one. The political decisions that seem so mundane and so bureaucratic at times are directly connected to the lives of each human being and therefore each one of those bureaucratic processes is central to the life and existence of each one of God's children. The more central a person is to politics, the more responsibility towards God such a person has. The higher a person is in the ecclesial ordering of things within churches and communities, the more responsibility towards a closer connection with God that person has. God is at the centre, and the public activity of each human being, be it religious or political, needs to be matched with and centred upon moments of contemplative emptiness together with the God who owns this planet and who ultimately remains at the beginning and at the end of human life.

In the case of Merton, we do not know what the impact of his Asian pilgrimage would have been on his own life, and this point has been a matter of speculation in many conferences and academic papers. I tend to agree with Judith Hunter when she argues that 'Had Merton lived, his natural tendency would have been to continue on, heading back into the woods, going "somewhere else developing a new way" . . .'[5] For the contemplatives who have been deeply immersed in the contemporary and in the world of the politics of God within human politics have perceived the world as always changing, realities as always embracing and the person in direct connection with God and his creation. This is the ongoing challenge: to transform Western individualism as the proper expression of the self, and include the possibility that at the centre of the human person there is a God who transforms the solely individual and public into a circular relationship between God–person–politics.

Robert Inchausti argues that in Merton's concrete contemplation, solitude and politics

> the world was not something static, a scholastic concept but an ever-changing, mutating, living reality, alive in his bloodstream. And when he described it, particularly in his poetry and later essays, it was always as a coparticipant, struggling to understand himself in and through the particulars of existence.[6]

That realization holds today for lay contemplatives and voters as we stand in the same ever-changing world with a sense of adventure, close to God but immersed within our world in contemplation, solitude and politics.

Towards a new contemplation

It is important to realize, as I close these pages of writing and reflection, that most people would admit that they seek some kind of spirituality, but many of them dislike organized religion or do not go to church within a contemporary secularized and autonomous Europe. This is God's world and therefore one must exercise respect towards those who believe in God yet do not form part of an 'established religion'. While exercising respect, one must learn from this experience that many do not find God in the Christian churches, and one must also exercise caution in assuming that one's way of approaching the divine or worshipping God is the only possible way.

It is important to realize that the experience of Christian contemplation and involvement in politics goes back 20 centuries, and that there have been many examples within the Christian Scriptures, the Christian tradition and the history of the Church. The development of an attitude in which the spiritual and the political, in which religion and politics are divided, has been a late development of Christian retreat due to the Enlightenment and the contradictions that many people found in a rational understanding of religion and science. Within those discussions there are, in my opinion, issues to be treated, but ultimately the involvement of God in his world, in his creation, has been systematic, active and loving. Regardless of evolution or the theological understanding by Israel of God's act of creation in the book of Genesis, chapters 1—2, the loving hand of a lover, of a friend and of a creator, has been with us since the early covenant of God with Abraham.

It is important to realize and accept that most probably the covenant with Abraham was a covenant with the human race, with all humans, with all stewards of creation and with all peoples and societies that were still to arise in the history of humanity. It is this God with whom we worship and communicate, it is this divine presence that we seek, it is the God of the poor and the marginalized who walks with us and with whom we fall in love. The God of sectarianism, discrimination and war does not exist – that image of God was left long ago with people who were not able to accept that the Christian God loves all and walks with all. It is possible that we have other ideas of God and that we reduce God to a smaller divine ally of a particular faction, group or community. However, at the end we only know that at Pentecost peoples of all nations, languages and races were called to accept the pouring out of the Spirit (Acts 2). What followed was not a sweet existence of communities that were looking inwards, but a missionary drive towards others and later persecution, the cross for Peter and, perhaps, Paul and a general sense of being outcast, poor and marginalized.

That is our destiny, and if we seek public recognition and the possibility of being accepted we have forgotten our roots: contemplative poor and politically marginalized communities at the periphery of things, in hope and love, hoping and loving with all. From contemplation to politics and back, we stand as Christians in the midst of a common humanity and must build on the values of the Kingdom of God that proclaim this inclusiveness against all discourses that speak of others as enemies and as different. In the words of Leonardo Boff:

We are currently at a crossroads in the history of humankind. We must create decentralized relations of power, relations that are egalitarian and inclusive, relations that are based on a deep concern for quality of life, so that all are able to feed themselves, to dwell with the minimum comfort, and attain knowledge and culture so that they are able to communicate with other human beings and preserve the integrity and beauty of nature.[7]

In practical terms, it is to return daily to contemplation and politics in order to experience God, the creator of a common humanity, of all creation and of all other human beings.

Notes

Introduction: issues in contemplation and politics today

1 The basic Christian communities that flourished in Latin America after the Second Vatican Council were formed by groups of Christians living in particular neighbourhoods, meeting regularly to pray, read the Scriptures and discuss their social engagement in their local areas, while taking care of the sick, the destitute and those without relatives.

2 Mario I. Aguilar, *The History and Politics of Latin American Theology*, vol. 1 (London: SCM Press), 2007.

3 See Michael S. Northcott, *An Angel Directs the Storm: Apocalyptic Religion and American Empire* (London and New York: I. B. Tauris), 2004.

4 Abbot Christopher Jamison, *Finding Sanctuary: Monastic Steps for Everyday Life* (London: Weidenfeld & Nicolson), 2006.

5 Thomas Merton, *Thomas Merton on St Bernard*, Cistercian Studies 9 (Kalamazoo, MI: Cistercian Publications; London and Oxford: A. R. Mowbray) 1980, p. 56.

6 James Conner OCSO, 'Thomas Merton and the Body of Christ', Closing homily – ITMS 10th General Meeting Christian Brothers University, Memphis, TN, 10 June 2007, *The Merton Seasonal* 32 (2007/3), pp. 15–17, at p. 15.

7 Athanasius, *The Life of Antony*, Classics of Western Spirituality (New York: Paulist Press), 1980; David Brakke, *Athanasius and Asceticism* (Baltimore, MD: Johns Hopkins Press), 1998; Samuel Rubenson, *The Letters of St Antony: Monasticism and the Making of a Saint* (Minneapolis, MS: Fortress Press), 1995.

8 Andrew Louth, *The Origins of the Christian Mystical Tradition* (Oxford: Clarendon Press), 1981.

9 Armand Veilleux (ed.), *Pachomian Koinonia: The Lives, Rules and Other Writings of Saint Pachomius*, Cistercian Studies 45–47 (Kalamazoo, MI: Cistercian Publications), 1980–2; Philip Rousseau, *Pachomius: The Making of a Community in Fourth Century Egypt* (Berkeley: University of California Press), 1999.

10 *Lives of the Desert Fathers* [*Historia Monachorum in Aegypto*], Cistercian Studies 34 (Kalamazoo, MI: Cistercian Publications), 1981; James E. Goehring, *Ascetics, Society and the Desert: Studies in Early Egyptian Monasticism* (Harrisburg, PA: Trinity Press International), 1999; Lucien Regnault, *The Day-To-Day Life of the Desert Fathers in Fourth-Century Egypt* (Petersham, MA: St Bede's), 1999; Graham E. Gould, *The Desert Fathers on Monastic Community* (New York: Oxford University Press), 1993.

11 Harriet A. Luckman and Linda Kulzer (eds), *Purity of Heart in Early Ascetic and Monastic Literature* (Collegeville, MN: The Liturgical Press), 1999; George Lawless, *Augustine of Hippo and His Monastic Rule* (New York: Oxford University Press), 1987; Conrad Leyser, *Authority and Asceticism from Augustine to Gregory the Great* (New York: Oxford University Press), 2001; Philip Rousseau, *Ascetics, Authority and the Church in the Age of Jerome and Cassian* (New York: Oxford University Press), 1978.

12 Henry Chadwick, *The Early Church: The Story of Emergent Christianity from the Apostolic Age to the Foundation of the Church of Rome*, The Pelican History of the Church 1 (London: Penguin), 1967, p. 178.

13 See, for example, David Brakke, *Demons and the Making of the Monk: Spiritual Combat in Early Christianity* (Cambridge, MA: Harvard University Press), 2006; Peter Brown, *The Body and Society: Men, Women and Sexual Renunciation in Early Christianity* (New York: Columbia University Press), 1988; Douglas Burton-Christie, *The Word in the Desert: Scripture and the Quest for Holiness in Early Christian Monasticism* (New York: Oxford University Press), 1993.

14 For a full survey, see Derwas Chitty, *The Desert a City* (Crestwood, NY: St Vladimir's Seminary Press), 1997; cf. William W. Johnston (ed.), *Encyclopedia of Monasticism*, 2 volumes (Chicago: Fitzroy Dearborn), 2000.

15 Marilyn Dunn, *The Emergence of Monasticism: From the Desert Fathers to the Early Middle Ages* (Oxford: Blackwell), 2000.

16 *The Rule of Benedict*, trans. Leonard Doyle (Collegeville, MN: Liturgical Press), 1980.

17 The Dalai Lama, *Freedom in Exile: The Autobiography of His Holiness The Dalai Lama of Tibet* (London: Hodder & Stoughton), 1990, p. 222.

18 William T. Cavanaugh, *Torture and Eucharist: Theology, Politics and the Body of Christ* (Oxford: Blackwell), 1998, p. 5.

1 Thomas Merton

1 For a history of the Abbey of Gethsemani, see Dianne Aprile, *The Abbey of Gethsemani: Place of Peace and Paradox* (Louisville, KY: Trout Lilly Press), 1998; for the history of the Cistercians, see Esther de Waal, *The Way of Simplicity: The Cistercian Tradition* (Maryknoll, NY: Orbis), 1998; James France, *The Cistercians in Medieval Art* (Kalamazoo, MI: Cistercian Publications), 1998; Louis Lekai, *The Cistercians: Ideals and Reality* (Kent, OH: Kent State University Press), 1977; André Louf, *The Cistercian Way* (Kalamazoo, MI: Cistercian Publications), 1983; Patricia Matarasso (ed.), *The Cistercian World: Monastic Writings of the Twelfth Century* (London: Penguin), 1993.

2 Regarding the issue of diverse biographies, it must be remembered that in 1967 Merton set up the Thomas Merton Legacy trust, a legal agreement that did not allow general access to Merton's diaries for 25 years, with the exception of the trustees: Naomi Burton Stone (his literary agent), James Laughlin (his publisher at New Directions) and Tommie O'Callaghan (Mrs Frank O'Callaghan); a few years later Robert Giroux replaced Stone within the board of trustees. An official biographer, John Howard Griffin, was appointed in 1969; however, he became ill, and in 1978 Michael Mott was appointed official biographer. He wrote the first biography of Merton, *The Seven Mountains of Thomas Merton* (Boston, MA: Houghton Mifflin), 1984, later published in the UK (London: Sheldon Press), 1986. Once all Merton's papers and diaries were available, a series of biographies followed, including Lawrence S. Cunningham, *Thomas Merton and the Monastic Vision* (Grand Rapids, MI: Eerdmans), 1999 and Monica Furlong, *Merton: A Biography* (London: Collins), 1980. A series of seven volumes of transcripts of Merton's diaries were published after Merton's moratorium ended (10 December 1993) – see 'Preface', in Patrick Hart OCSO (ed.), *Run to the Mountain: The Story of a Vocation – The Journals of Thomas Merton, Volume One, 1939–1941* (New York: HarperCollins and HarperSanFrancisco), 1996, p. xi.

3 Merton's memories of his mother were that she was strict, and according to Monica Furlong, 'there is always a faint bitterness in his references to her; she seemed critical, pedagogic, "severe", measuring him all the time against some standard that seemed unattainable, leaving him with a sour taste of failure, and of

being inadequate.' See Furlong, *Merton: A Biography*, pp. 13–15, at p. 15.

4 Mott, *Seven Mountains of Thomas Merton*, pp. 50–2.

5 Thomas Merton, *The Seven Storey Mountain* (London: SPCK) 1990, pp. 71–2.

6 Merton, *Seven Storey Mountain*, pp. 199–225.

7 Merton had attended some of those Communist meetings and at one of them had signed as a member of the Young Communist League, taking the party name Frank Swift; Furlong, *Merton: A Biography*, p. 67.

8 Furlong, *Merton: A Biography*, p. 67.

9 Even after years in Gethsemani, Merton followed Maritain's writings and life – see Merton's diary entry for 23 October 1963: 'The rumour goes around that Maritain has been made a Cardinal. John Howard Griffin even declares he has seen this in print', in Robert E. Daggy (ed.), *Dancing in the Water of Life: Seeking Peace in the Hermitage – The Journals of Thomas Merton, Volume Five, 1963–1965* (New York: HarperCollins and HarperSanFrancisco), 1997, p. 26.

10 Merton, *Seven Storey Mountain*, p. 316.

11 Merton had been previously rejected as a conscript because of his teeth, but owing to the impending conflict with Japan the US Army was drafting thousands of young Americans, and the local secretary of the draft board told him that under the new pressures he most probably would be drafted into the army – see Mott, *Seven Mountains of Thomas Merton*, p. 200.

12 Merton, *Seven Storey Mountain*, p. 378.

13 Cunningham, *Thomas Merton and the Monastic Vision*, p. 22.

14 Wednesday in Holy Week, 9 April 1941, at Our Lady of Gethsemani, in Hart (ed.), *Run to the Mountain*, p. 340.

15 Merton published a history of his religious order under the title *The Waters of Siloe* (New York: Harcourt Brace), 1949.

16 Thomas Merton, *The Sign of Jonas* (San Diego, CA, New York and London: Harcourt Brace), 1979.

17 Merton, *Sign of Jonas*, p. 361.

18 Thomas Merton, *Conjectures of a Guilty Bystander* (New York: Doubleday), 1966.

19 Lawrence S. Cunningham, 'Introduction', in Lawrence S. Cunningham (ed.), *A Search for Solitude: Pursuing the Monk's True Life – The Journals of Thomas Merton, Volume Three, 1952–1960* (New York: HarperCollins and HarperSanFrancisco), 1996, p. xvi.

20 See 'Some Bibliographical Notes' in Cunningham, *Thomas Merton and the Monastic Vision*, pp. 211–25.

21 The letter was signed by Cardinals Valerio Valeri (Cardinal Prefect) and Larraona. Merton wrote in his diary: 'And they agreed with my superiors that I did not have an eremitical vocation. That therefore what they asked of me was to stay in the monastery where God had put me, and I would find interior solitude', 17 December 1959, in Cunningham (ed.), *Search for Solitude*, p. 358.

22 See, for example, Thomas Merton, *Contemplative Prayer* (London: Darton, Longman & Todd), 2005.

23 17–18 August 1965, in Daggy (ed.), *Dancing in the Water of Life*, pp. 280–1.

24 25 August 1965 in Daggy (ed.), *Dancing in the Water of Life*, p. 283.

25 For example, on 25 September 1965 he wrote: 'The sun came up in mist and as I was finishing my wood chopping the house was steaming like a big contented beast. The sun was warm but tonight promises to be cold again', in Daggy (ed.), *Dancing in the Water of Life*, p. 299.

26 See Christine M. Bochen (ed.), *Learning To Love: Exploring Solitude and Freedom – The Journals of Thomas Merton, Volume Six, 1966–1967* (New York: HarperCollins and HarperSanFrancisco), 1997.

27 Mott, *Seven Mountains of Thomas Merton*, p. 458.

28 Merton wrote: 'it has become "normal" to regard war – any war demanded by the military – as Christian duty, Christian love, Christian virtue, that a few like the Berrigans, in their desperation, try to show by extreme protest that it is not normal at all', Circular Letter to Friends, midsummer 1968, in Robert E. Daggy (ed.), *Thomas Merton: The Road to Joy – The Letters of Thomas Merton to New and Old Friends* (New York: Farrar, Straus & Giroux), 1989, p. 116. Daniel Berrigan's visit was reported in a letter to Sister Therese Lentfoehr SDS, 20 September 1962; see Circular Letter to Friends, midsummer 1968, in Daggy (ed.), *Thomas Merton: The Road to Joy*, p. 241.

29 Thomas Merton, Circular Letter to Friends, midsummer 1968, in Daggy (ed.), *Thomas Merton: The Road to Joy*, p. 116.

30 Letters to Sister Therese Lentfoehr SDS, 20 December 1962 and 19 February 1963, in Daggy (ed.), *Thomas Merton: The Road to Joy*, p. 243.

31 On hearing the news of Merton's death, Dan Berrigan 'wept inconsolably for his dear friend and teacher'; in Murray Polner and Jim O'Grady, *Disarmed and Dangerous: The Radical Lives and Times of Daniel and Philip Berrigan* (New York: Basic Books), 1997, p. 211.

32 Merton had certainly been shocked and ready to withdraw any support for the anti-war movement when, on 9 November 1965, Roger LaPorte, 21 years of age, stood in front of the United Nations building in New York and after dousing himself with petrol set himself ablaze. Merton sent a telegram withdrawing support for the Catholic Peace Fellowship; however, later on he thought he had been too hard and continued supporting the movement – see 11 November 1965, in Daggy (ed.), *Dancing in the Water of Life*, p. 314.

33 See Christine M. Bochen (ed.), *Thomas Merton: The Courage for Truth – The Letters of Thomas Merton to Writers* (New York: Farrar, Straus & Giroux), 1993.

34 Thomas Merton to Nicanor Parra, 28 April 1967, in Bochen (ed.), *Thomas Merton: The Courage for Truth*, p. 214.

35 Brother Patrick Hart, 'Foreword', in Naomi Burton Stone, Brother Patrick Hart and James Laughlin (eds), *The Asian Journal of Thomas Merton* (New York: New Directions), 1975, p. xxiii.

36 During the 1960s Merton had corresponded with many scholars of Hinduism and Buddhism – see, for example, William Apel, 'There Comes a Time: The Interfaith Letters of Thomas Merton and Dona Luisa Coomaraswamy', *The Merton Journal* 13, (2006/2); William Apel, *Signs of Peace: The Interfaith Letters of Thomas Merton* (Maryknoll, NY: Orbis), 2006; and Letters to Sister Therese Lentfoehr SDS, 20 December 1962 and 19 February 1963, in Daggy (ed.), *Thomas Merton: The Road to Joy*, pp. 242–4, at p. 243.

37 *Asian Journal of Thomas Merton*.

38 The Fourteenth Dalai Lama, Tenzin Gyatso, was born into a peasant family in Amdo, eastern Tibet in 1935, and after being identified as the incarnation of the previous Dalai Lama at the age of two, was moved to Lhasa at the age of four. With the Chinese occupation of Tibet the political situation changed, and after the Tibetan National Uprising on 10 March 1959, the Dalai Lama left Tibet and moved to India, where he was granted refugee status. Over the years, thousands of Tibetan refugees crossed into India, and the Dalai Lama managed to establish monasteries as well as

his government in Dharamsala, where he met Merton in 1968. For a detailed account of the Dalai Lama's life, see Michael Harris Goodman, *The Last Dalai Lama: A Biography* (London: Sidgwick & Jackson), 1986.

39 See Thomas Merton, 'November circular letter to friends', New Delhi, India, 9 November 1968, published as 'Appendix VI', in *Asian Journal of Thomas Merton*, pp. 320–5; Merton's visit is also mentioned in Goodman, *Last Dalai Lama*, p. 325.

40 'November 4, afternoon', in *Asian Journal of Thomas Merton*, pp. 100–2.

41 *Asian Journal of Thomas Merton*, pp. 112–13.

42 *Asian Journal of Thomas Merton*, p. 112.

43 *Asian Journal of Thomas Merton*, p. 113.

44 *Asian Journal of Thomas Merton*, pp. 124–5.

45 *Asian Journal of Thomas Merton*, p. 125. On the Dalai Lama and Marxism, see The Fourteenth Dalai Lama, *Freedom in Exile: The Autobiography of His Holiness the Dalai Lama of Tibet* (London: Hodder & Stoughton), 1990, pp. 98–9, 251, particularly p. 296, where he confesses that 'in as much as I have any political allegiance, I suppose I am still half Marxist', and 'the other attractive thing about Marxism for me is its assertion that man is ultimately responsible for his own destiny. This reflects Buddhist thought exactly.'

46 The Dalai Lama writes about 'Father Thomas Merton, the American Benedictine Monk', see The Fourteenth Dalai Lama, *Freedom in Exile*, pp. 207–8. See also Joseph Quinn Raab, 'Comrades for Peace: Thomas Merton, The Dalai Lama and the Preferential Option for Nonviolence', in Victor A. Kramer and David Belcastro (eds), *The Merton Annual: Studies in Culture, Spirituality and Social Concerns* 19 (Louisville, KY: Fons Vitae), 2007, pp. 255–66.

47 The text of the lecture is available as 'Appendix VII' in *Asian Journal of Thomas Merton*, pp. 326–43.

48 *Asian Journal of Thomas Merton*, p. 327.

49 *Asian Journal of Thomas Merton*, p. 330 (Feuerbach's original is, '*Der Mensch ist, was er ißt*').

50 *Asian Journal of Thomas Merton*, p. 341.

51 *Asian Journal of Thomas Merton*, p. 343.

52 Letter from Six Trappist Delegates to Abbot Flavian Burns, Sawang Kaniwat, Bangkok, 11 December 1968, published as 'Appendix VIII' in *Asian Journal of Thomas Merton*, pp. 344–7.

2 Ernesto Cardenal

1 Teófilo Cabestrero, *Ministers of God, Ministers of the People: Testimonies of Faith from Nicaragua* (Maryknoll, NY: Orbis; London: Zed), 1983.

2 Ernesto Cardenal, *La Revolución Perdida: Memorias*, vol. 3 (Mexico City: Fondo De Cultura Económica), 2005, pp. 288–301.

3 I have outlined the history of Nicaragua and Cardenal's history in Mario I. Aguilar, *The History and Politics of Latin American Theology*, vol. 1 (London: SCM Press), 2007, ch. 5.

4 Nicaragua has always been a very literate society, and the influence of poets has been central to national developments – see Thomas W. Walker, *Nicaragua: The Land of Sandino* (Boulder, CO and London: Westview Press), 2nd edn, 1986, pp. 76–7. The same can be said of the influence of left-wing poets within the different periods of possible liberation from oppression – see Bridget Albaraca, Edward Baker, Ileana Rodríguez and Marc Zimmerman (eds), *Nicaragua in Revolution: The Poets Speak/ Nicaragua en Revolución: Los Poetas Hablan* (Minneapolis, MN: Marxist Educational Press), 1980.

5 Cardenal asserted: 'Mi principal influencia y mi principal maestro ha sido Ezra Pound', in José Luis González-Balado, *Ernesto Cardenal: Poeta Revolucionario Monje* (Salamanca: Ediciones Sígueme, 1978), p. 58. Ezra Pound (1885–1972) wrote particular aesthetic constructions that included historical assertions in his *Cantos*, and also campaigned for the non-intervention of the USA in Italy during World War Two – see Ira B. Nadel, *Ezra Pound: A Literary Life* (Houndmills: Macmillan; New York: Palgrave), 2004.

6 For a comparative textual analysis of Ezra Pound and Cardenal, see Eduardo Urdanivia Bertarelli, *La Poesía de Ernesto Cardenal: Cristianismo y Revolución* (Lima: Latinoamericana Editores), 1984, pp. 29–50.

7 Ernesto Cardenal, *Poesía y Revolución: Antología Poética* (Mexico City: Editorial Edicol), 1979, pp. 11–25.

8 Ernesto Cardenal, *Vida perdida: Memorias I* (Madrid: Editorial Trotta), 2005, pp. 99, 102.

9 See Jim Forest, *Living with Wisdom: A Life of Thomas Merton* (Maryknoll, NY: Orbis), 1991, p. 79. Cardenal's new name was given in Latin as Laurentius; however, Merton used the Spanish, Lorenzo, and reminded Cardenal that it was the name of a great writer: D. H. Lawrence. See Cardenal, *Vida perdida*, p. 105.

10 After his departure from Nicaragua, Cardenal's friend Pablo Antonio Cuadra dedicated almost all the literary section of the newspaper *La Prensa* to him – see Cardenal, *Vida perdida*, p. 116.

11 Cardenal, *Vida perdida*, p. 14.

12 Forest, *Living with Wisdom*, pp. 79–80.

13 Cardenal, *Vida perdida*, pp. 106–7.

14 Cardenal, *Vida perdida*, p. 110.

15 Cardenal, *Vida perdida*, p. 112, cf. 137–41; at that time Cardenal's brother, Fernando, was studying for the priesthood in Ecuador, and Merton also asked Ernesto Cardenal to enquire about possible locations for a monastery in Ecuador – Cardenal, *Vida perdida*, pp. 124–5.

16 Cardenal, *Vida perdida*, p. 128.

17 Cardenal, *Vida perdida*, p. 142.

18 *The Rule of Saint Benedict*, trans. Leonard Doyle (Collegeville, MN: Liturgical Press), 2001.

19 Cardenal, *Vida perdida*, pp. 129–30.

20 Cardenal, *Vida perdida*, pp. 145–6.

21 Cardenal, *Vida perdida*, p. 159.

22 Cardenal, *Vida perdida*, pp. 174–5.

23 Cardenal, *Vida perdida*, p. 176.

24 Letter from Thomas Merton to Archbishop Larraona, Head of the Sacred Congregation of Religious at the Vatican, 8 September 1959, in William H. Shannon (ed.), *Witness to Freedom: The Letters of Thomas Merton in Times of Crisis* (New York: Farrar, Straus & Giroux), 1994, pp. 205–7.

25 Cardenal, *Vida perdida*, p. 179.

26 Letter from Thomas Merton to Father Jean Daniélou, 5 December 1959, in Shannon (ed.), *Witness to Freedom*, pp. 209–11.

27 Cardenal, *Vida perdida*, p. 284.

28 Letter from Thomas Merton to Ernesto Cardenal, 8 October 1959, in Shannon (ed.), *Witness to Freedom*, pp. 207–9.

29 Cardenal, *Vida perdida*, pp. 263–4; Letter from Thomas Merton to Dom Gregorio Lemercier, 17 December 1959, in Shannon (ed.), *Witness to Freedom*, pp. 211–14.

30 Letter from Thomas Merton to Dom James Fox, 17 December 1959, in Shannon (ed.), *Witness to Freedom*, pp. 214–16.

31 Letter from Thomas Merton to Valerio Cardinal Valeri, 2 January 1960, in Shannon (ed.), *Witness to Freedom*, pp. 216–19.

32 Letter from Thomas Merton to Father Jean Daniélou, 2 January 1960, in Shannon (ed.), *Witness to Freedom*, pp. 219–21.

33 Cardenal, *Vida perdida*, p. 283.
34 In Brazil, for example, Bishop Pedro Casaldáliga, when arrested, was questioned about his possession of a Portuguese translation of *Salmos*, and the book was declared forbidden in Nicaragua – see Ernesto Cardenal, 'Epístola a Monseñor Casaldáliga', in Cardenal, *Poesía y Revolución*, p. 133.
35 For analyses of Cardenal's psalms, see José Promis Ojeda, 'Espíritu y Materia: Los "salmos" de Ernesto Cardenal', and Lidia Dapaz Strout, 'Nuevos cantos de vida y esperanza: Los Salmos de Cardenal y la nueva ética', in *Ernesto Cardenal: Poeta de la Liberación Latinoamericana* (Buenos Aires: Fernando García Cambeiro), 1975, pp. 15–38, 107–31.
36 On 17 March 1994, Ernesto Cardenal sent the editor of Merton's letters three letters that had been given to him by Merton in October 1965 during his visit to Gethsemani. One was addressed to Cardenal, the second to the Sacred Congregation of Religious in Rome and the third to Pope Paul VI. They were to be sent when and if Merton wanted, and Cardenal suspected that due to his death Merton never had the chance to instruct him to do so. The three letters supported Cardenal's foundation of a monastery in Nicaragua, and spoke of the urgent need for contemplative life in Latin America – see Letter from Thomas Merton to Ernesto Cardenal, 22 October 1965, Letter from Thomas Merton to the Most Rev. Archbishop Paul Philippe and Letter from Thomas Merton to His Holiness Pope Paul VI, in Shannon (ed.), *Witness to Freedom*, pp. 227–30.
37 The archipelago of Solentiname has 30 islands, and at that time there were around 1,000 people or nearly 90 families. Cardenal's lay monastery was located on the largest island, Mancarrón.
38 Claribel Alegría and D. J. Flakoll, *Nicaragua: La Revolución Sandinista – Una crónica política 1855–1979* (Mexico DF: Ediciones Era), 1982, p. 274.
39 'I came to Solentiname in order to flee from what Christians call the world, that lately includes capitalism and the consumer society. I came to this island searching for solitude, silence, meditation, and ultimately searching for God. God brought me to others. Contemplation led me to revolution. As I have said before, it was not the reading of Marx that led me to revolution but the reading of the gospel', in Spanish in González-Balado, *Ernesto Cardenal*, p. 152 (my translation).

40 Ernesto Cardenal, *El Evangelio en Solentiname*, vol. 1 (Salamanca: Ediciones Sígueme), 1976, and *El Evangelio en Solentiname*, vol. 2 (Salamanca: Ediciones Sígueme), 1978.

41 Cardenal, 'Introducción', in *El Evangelio en Solentiname*, vol. 1, pp. 9–10.

42 Cardenal, *El Evangelio en Solentiname*, vol. 2, pp. 143–7.

43 Cardenal, *El Evangelio en Solentiname*, vol. 2, pp. 143–4.

44 Cardenal, *El Evangelio en Solentiname*, vol. 2, pp. 144–5. Cardenal gives only the Christian names of these two contributors.

45 Cardenal, *El Evangelio en Solentiname*, vol. 2, pp. 145–6.

46 Cardenal, *El Evangelio en Solentiname*, vol. 2, pp. 146–7.

47 Peter Wright, 'Introduction', in *The Peasant Poets of Solentiname*, trans. Peter Wright (London: Katabasis), 1991, pp. 1–7.

48 *Peasant Poets of Solentiname*.

49 'El ataque a San Carlos', in Alegría and Flakoll, *Nicaragua: La Revolución Sandinista*, pp. 274–91. Some of the young poets were also involved in the attack on the San Carlos barracks.

50 Dinah Livingstone, 'Introduction', in *Nicaraguan New Time: Poems by Ernesto Cardenal*, trans. Dinah Livingstone (London: Journeyman), 1998, pp. 11–19, at p. 16.

51 Ernesto Cardenal, 'For Those Dead Our Dead', in *Nicaraguan New Time*, p. 89.

52 Dinah Livingstone, 'Introduction', in Ernesto Cardenal, *The Music of the Spheres*, trans. Dinah Livingstone (London: Katabasis), 1990, pp. 5–11, at p. 5.

53 Cardenal, *Music of the Spheres*, p. 15.

3 Daniel Berrigan SJ

1 For a history of the Vietnam War, see Stanley Karnow, *Vietnam: A History* (London: Pimlico), revised edn, 1994.

2 Important works on the history of the Berrigan family and Daniel Berrigan's life are: Murray Polner and Jim O'Grady, *Disarmed and Dangerous: The Radical Lives and Times of Daniel and Philip Berrigan* (New York: Basic Books), 1997; Daniel Berrigan, *To Dwell in Peace, An Autobiography* (San Francisco: Harper & Row), 1987; and John Dear (ed.), *Apostle of Peace: Essays in Honor of Daniel Berrigan* (Maryknoll, NY: Orbis), 1996.

3 Important dates in the history of the Jesuits include: 27 September 1540, when Pope Paul III issued the papal bull *Regimini militantis Ecclesiae*, which authorized the existence of

the Society of Jesus, a few years before the Council of Trent (1545–63); 21 July 1550, when Pope Julius III issued the bull *Exposcit debitum*, which approved the constitutions of the Society of Jesus, a document that had been drafted by Ignatius; and 1622, when Pope Gregory XV canonized Ignatius of Loyola and his companion Francis Xavier, missionary to Asia.

4 In 1939 there were 6,000 Jesuits in the USA, more than 20 per cent of the total number of Jesuits in the world before World War Two.

5 There is no doubt that the *Spiritual Exercises* are central to the formation and spiritual growth of a Jesuit, not only because they were given by Ignatius to all his companions and followers, but because the spiritual movement within the *Exercises* makes a Jesuit now as it did in the past. The striking reality of the life of a Jesuit is that all Jesuits throughout the ages have had the experience of the *Exercises*, and from that experience of 30 days in prayer with the help of a director, they continue searching for Christ and for his will throughout every period of their lives. The *Exercises* were written by Ignatius during his deep spiritual experience of conversion at Manresa (1521–2), and later those drafts were finalized and edited while he was a student in Paris – see contemporary text published as W. H. Longridge, *The Spiritual Exercises of Saint Ignatius of Loyola*, translated from the Spanish with a commentary and a translation of the *Directorium in Exercitia* (London: Robert Scott), 1919. His reflections were not intended as a pious book to be read by others for personal inspiration, but as a guide for spiritual directors of others who were seeking God and seeking a personal conversion. During his arrests and interrogation by the Inquisition, Ignatius maintained that he was guiding others towards God, not towards himself, and that the *Exercises* guided his structuring of a deep reflection on his own experience of conversion. The *Exercises* became a path to inner conversion but at the same time a marker of identity. If you were to become a Jesuit it was not sufficient to have a vocation to the religious life or to the priesthood, but you should pass through a rite of passage marked by the experience of God through the *Exercises*. For the history of the Jesuits, see John W. O'Malley, *The First Jesuits* (Cambridge, MA and London: Harvard University Press), 1993, and for a particular view of the Jesuits in Latin America, see Mario I. Aguilar, *The History and Politics of Latin American Theology*, vol. 2 (London: SCM Press), 2008, ch. 4. Thus, over the centuries Jesuit novices and seasoned Jesuits have

gone through the *Exercises* not only once but several times during their lifetime. In the contemporary life of the Jesuits, novices go through the *Exercises* during the first spiritual steps of their Jesuit life and once again during their tertiary period, a period of discernment and renewed apostolic zeal before their final religious profession as Jesuits for life, some 15 years or so after their first profession after their novitiate. These norms and practices were revised by the 34th General Congregation of the Jesuits in 1995.

6 John Petrie (ed.), *The Worker-priests: A Collective Documentation* (London: Routledge & Kegan Paul), 1956, p. xi.

7 The Josephites were founded in England in 1866 with the intention of serving black Catholics. The congregation moved to the USA in 1871 as four priests arrived to minister to freed slaves. By 1965 there were 250 Josephite priests and brothers – see Stephen J. Ochs, *Desegregating the Altar: The Josephites and the Struggle for Black Priests, 1871–1960* (Baton Rouge: Louisiana State University Press), 1990. It is possible to argue that a more thorough piece of research on contemplation and politics should include Daniel and Philip Berrigan side by side. However, I have chosen to deal mainly with Daniel Berrigan's life because he shared with his brother Philip the same intense commitment to peace and justice but was a writer, poet and contemplative in his own right who remained a Jesuit and a priest, thus exercising a greater influence within twentieth-century American Catholicism. Philip Berrigan (1923–2002) was ordained as a Josephite priest in late spring 1955, at a liturgical celebration that took place at the Shrine of the Immaculate Conception in Washington, DC, and immediately took up his ministry as assistant pastor at Our Lady of Perpetual Help parish in the Anacostia district, working with poor African Americans – see Polner and O'Grady, *Disarmed and Dangerous*, p. 95. In 1970, Philip Berrigan married Elizabeth McAlister, an activist sister of the Sacred Heart of Mary; they had three children – see Philip Berrigan and Elizabeth McAlister, *The Time's Discipline: The Beatitudes and Nuclear Resistance* (Baltimore, MD: Fortkamp), 1989 and Philip Berrigan with Fred A. Wilcox, *Fighting the Lamb's War: Skirmishes with the American Empire* (Monroe, ME: Common Courage Press), 1996.

8 Robert E. Daggy (ed.), *Dancing in the Water of Life: Seeking Peace in the Hermitage – The Journals of Thomas Merton, Volume Five, 1963–1965* (New York: HarperCollins and HarperSanFrancisco), 1997, p. 253.

9 Polner and O'Grady, *Disarmed and Dangerous*, p. 107. According to Merton's diary, the retreat took place in November 1964 rather than March 1965, as reported by Polner and O'Grady – see entries for 17 and 19 November 1964 in Daggy (ed.), *Dancing in the Water of Life*, pp. 167–8.

10 Michael Mott, *The Seven Mountains of Thomas Merton* (London: Sheldon Press), 1986, pp. 406–7.

11 Mott, *Seven Mountains of Thomas Merton*, p. 407.

12 Paul R. Dekar, 'Thomas Merton, Gandhi, the "Uprising" of Youth in the '60s, and Building Non-Violent Movements Today', *The Merton Seasonal* 31, 4, 2006, pp. 16–23, at p. 21.

13 The first Buddhist monk to immolate himself was Quang Duc, a 62-year-old, in the streets of Saigon in 1963; he left a note requesting from the authorities 'charity and compassion'.

14 Merton's diary entry for 7 November 1965, in Daggy (ed.), *Dancing in the Water of Life*, p. 313.

15 Westmoreland requested three 'force packages': 108,000 for Vietnam to arrive on 1 May 1968, the rest to be assigned in September or December, even kept in the USA if there was a shortage of troops – see Karnow, *Vietnam*, p. 564.

16 Patrick O'Brien, 'Introduction', in Daniel Berrigan, *Tulips in the Prison Yard: Selected Poems of Daniel Berrigan* (Dublin: Dedalus Press), 1992, pp. 7–11, at p. 9.

17 Polner and O'Grady, *Disarmed and Dangerous*, p. 202.

18 Harvey Cox, 'Tongues of Flame: The Trial of the Catonsville Nine', in Stephen Halpert and Tom Murray (eds), *The Witness of the Berrigans* (New York: Doubleday), 1972, pp. 22–3.

19 Daniel Berrigan, *The Trial of the Catonsville Nine* (Boston, MA: Beacon Press), 1970.

20 Daniel Berrigan, *And the Risen Bread: Selected Poems 1957–1997* (New York: Fordham University Press), 1998.

21 Daniel Berrigan, *Lamentations: From New York to Kabul and Beyond* (Lanham, MD and Chicago: Sheed & Ward), 2002.

22 Colleen Kelly, 'Foreword', in Berrigan, *Lamentations*, pp. xi–xiv, at p. xii.

23 Kelly, 'Foreword'.

24 Berrigan, *Lamentations*, p. xviii.

25 Daniel Berrigan, *Daniel: Under the Siege of the Divine* (Farmington, PA and Robertsbridge, E. Sussex: The Plough Publishing House of the Bruderhof Foundation), 1998, p. x.

26 'Holy Martyr Rutilio Grande SJ and the Holy Child of El Salvador', in Daniel Berrigan, with icons by William Hart McNichols, *The Bride: Images of the Church* (Maryknoll, NY: Orbis), 2000, pp. 113–17, at p. 117.

27 Alistair Kee, 'The Criticism of the Spirit', in Alistair Kee (ed.), *Seeds of Liberation: Spiritual Dimensions to Political Struggle* (London: SCM Press), 1973, pp. 3–6, at p. 4.

28 'Property – Discussion with Dan Berrigan', in Alistair Kee (ed.), *Seeds of Liberation*, pp. 68–71, at p. 69.

4 Sheila Cassidy

1 Michael Hollings, 'Introduction', in Sheila Cassidy, *Audacity to Believe* (London: Darton, Longman & Todd), 1992, pp. xi–xiv, at p. xiii.

2 See Sheila Cassidy, *Made for Laughter* (London: Darton, Longman & Todd), 2006 and *Audacity to Believe*.

3 Cassidy, *Made for Laughter*, p. 211.

4 Cassidy, *Made for Laughter*, p. 8.

5 Cassidy, *Audacity to Believe*, p. 5.

6 See Mario I. Aguilar, *A Social History of the Catholic Church in Chile I: The First Period of the Pinochet Government 1973–1980* (Lewiston, NY, Queenston, Ontario and Lampeter, Wales: Edwin Mellen Press), 2004, pp. 96–101.

7 See Mario I. Aguilar, *A Social History of the Catholic Church in Chile IV: Torture and Forced Disappearance 1973–1974* (Lewiston, NY, Queenston, Ontario and Lampeter, Wales: Edwin Mellen Press), 2008.

8 See Mario I. Aguilar, *A Social History of the Catholic Church in Chile II: The Pinochet Government and Cardinal Silva Henríquez* (Lewiston, NY, Queenston, Ontario and Lampeter, Wales: Edwin Mellen Press), 2006, pp. 263–5.

9 Silva Henríquez wrote: 'I was told many times that I was naive, that we confused charity with ignorance, that the terrorists would not spare us. I always answered that in a situation where a priest witnesses a human being who doesn't have an exit, who is persecuted and wounded, the priest is not encountering a manifestation of terrorism, an abstract concept, but instead is faced with human pain, a pain that we must redeem, because it was for this purpose that Christ instituted the Church on earth.' Cardinal

Raúl Silva Henríquez, *Memorias III* (Santiago, Ediciones Copygraph), p. 77 (my translation).

10 Henríquez, *Memorias III*, p. 82.

11 Cassidy, *Audacity to Believe*, p. 156.

12 Eugenio Ahumada, Rodrigo Atria, Javier Luis Egaña, Augusto Góngora, Carmen Quesney, Gustavo Saball and Gustavo Villalobos, *Chile: La Memoria Prohibida II* (Santiago: Pehuén), 1989, p. 174. See the whole narrative at pp. 170–87.

13 Cassidy, *Audacity to Believe*, p. 157.

14 Cassidy, *Audacity to Believe*, pp. 162–3.

15 Ascanio Cavallo, Manuel Salazar and Oscar Sepúlveda, *La historia oculta del régimen militar: Memoria de una época 1973–1988* (Santiago: Grijalbo), 1997, p. 91.

16 Most prisoners who were brought to the Villa Grimaldi recalled the vehicle stopping and then the metallic noise of a large steel door being opened. With the advent of democracy in Chile, a symbolic act came about in which relatives of those who had disappeared from the Villa Grimaldi opened the gates for the whole world to visit. Today, the Villa Grimaldi has been transformed into a Park for Peace, with guided tours on the history of the torture camp.

17 Cassidy, *Audacity to Believe*, p. 172.

18 Cassidy, *Audacity to Believe*, p. 175.

19 Cassidy, *Audacity to Believe*, p. 194.

20 Cassidy, *Audacity to Believe*, p. 220.

21 Cassidy, *Audacity to Believe*, pp. 224–5.

22 Cassidy, *Audacity to Believe*, p. 230.

23 Cassidy, *Audacity to Believe*, pp. 247–8.

24 Cassidy, *Audacity to Believe*, p. 258.

25 Cassidy, *Audacity to Believe*, p. 285.

26 Cassidy, *Audacity to Believe*, pp. 297–8.

27 Cassidy, *Audacity to Believe*, p. 300.

28 Jorge Hourton (Vicario Zona Norte), 'Adiós a la Dra. Sheila Cassidy', *Comunidad Cristiana – Iglesia de Santiago*, 11 January 1976, in Cassidy, *Audacity to Believe*, p. 334.

29 Cassidy, *Made for Laughter*, pp. 100–30.

30 Cassidy, *Made for Laughter*, pp. 131–211.

5 Archbishop Desmond Tutu

1 Desmond Tutu, '1984 Nobel Lecture', text avalable in John Allen (ed.), *Archbishop Desmond Tutu: The Rainbow People of*

God (London and New York: Doubleday), 1994, pp. 84–92, at p. 92.

2 John Allen, 'A Growing Nightmarish Fear (1976)', in Allen (ed.), *Archbishop Desmond Tutu*, pp. 4–5.

3 Allen, 'A Growing Nightmarish Fear', p. 4.

4 On 2 July 1955, he married Leah Nomalizo Tutu. They had four children.

5 See Shirley du Boulay, *Tutu: Voice of the Voiceless* (London: Penguin), 1989; Allister Sparks, *The Mind of South Africa* (New York: Knopf), 1990; Tore Frängsmyr (editor-in-charge) and Irwin Abrams (ed.), *From Nobel Lectures: Peace 1981–1990* (Singapore: World Scientific Publishing), 1997.

6 Desmond Tutu to The Hon Prime Minister John Vorster, 6 May 1976, text available in Allen (ed.), *Archbishop Desmond Tutu*, pp. 7–14.

7 Desmond Tutu to The Hon Prime Minister John Vorster, 6 May 1976, text available in Allen (ed.), *Archbishop Desmond Tutu*, p. 11.

8 See Desmond Tutu, *Crying in the Wilderness* (Oxford: A. R. Mowbray), 1986.

9 See Monica Wilson and Leonard Thompson (eds), *The Oxford History of South Africa, vol. II: South Africa 1870–1966* (London: Oxford University Press), 1971.

10 See Francis Meli, *A History of the ANC: South Africa Belongs To Us* (London: James Currey), 1988.

11 Allen (ed.), *Archbishop Desmond Tutu*, p. 15.

12 See Steve Biko (ed. Aelred Stubbs CR), *I Write What I Like* (New York: Harper & Row), 1978.

13 Desmond Tutu, 'Oh God, How Long Can We Go On? (1977)', in Allen (ed.), *Archbishop Desmond Tutu*, pp. 17–21, at p. 21.

14 For an analysis of the 1970s in South Africa, see John W. De Gruchy, *The Church Struggle in South Africa* (Grand Rapids, MI: Eerdmans), 1979. For a theoretical treatment of the changing relations between the churches and the South African state, see Charles Villa-Vicencio, *Trapped in Apartheid: A Socio-Theological History of the English-Speaking Churches* (Maryknoll, NY: Orbis), 1988, and *Civil Disobedience and Beyond: Law, Resistance and Religion in South Africa* (Grand Rapids, MI: Eerdmans), 1990.

15 For a history of the SACC and the development of the different Christian traditions in South Africa, see Marjorie Hope and James Young, *The South African Churches in a Revolutionary Situation* (Maryknoll, NY: Orbis), 1981.

16 The World Alliance of Reformed Churches General Council meeting in Ottawa, 25 August 1982, endorsed many other previous declarations by national reformed bodies, and reiterated 'its firm conviction that apartheid ("separate development") is sinful and incompatible with the Gospel' – see 'Racism and South Africa: Statement adopted by the General Council in Ottawa on 25 August 1982', II.1, full statement in John Gruchy and Charles Villa-Vicencio (eds), *Apartheid is a Heresy* (Cape Town: David Philip; Guildford: Lutterworth), 1983, pp. 168–73.

17 On complex ruptures within Christianity in South Africa, see John W. De Gruchy, 'Grappling with a Colonial Heritage: the English-speaking Churches under imperialism and apartheid', in Richard Elphick and Rodney Davenport (eds), *Christianity in South Africa: A Political, Social and Cultural History* (Cape Town: David Philip; Berkeley: University of California Press; Oxford: James Currey), 1997, pp. 155–72.

18 Allen (ed.), *Archbishop Desmond Tutu*, p. 26.

19 'We drink water to fill our stomachs: address to the Provincial Synod of the Church of the Province of Southern Africa, 1979', text available in Allen (ed.), *Archbishop Desmond Tutu*, pp. 27–41, at p. 31.

20 Desmond Tutu, 'A deep and passionate love for our land: transcript of remarks to P. W. Botha and members of his cabinet, 1980', text available in Allen (ed.), *Archbishop Desmond Tutu*, pp. 43–6, at pp. 44–5.

21 Desmond Tutu, 'Why did Mr. Botha's courage fail him? – Extract from a presentation to a Johannesburg study group, 1981', text available in Allen (ed.), *Archbishop Desmond Tutu*, pp. 47–52, at p. 50.

22 Desmond Tutu, 'The Divine Imperative, 1982', text available in Allen (ed.), *Archbishop Desmond Tutu*, pp. 53–78, at p. 58.

23 Desmond Tutu, 'Not Even Invited to the Party, 1983', text available in Allen (ed.), *Archbishop Desmond Tutu*, pp. 79–82.

24 Desmond Tutu, '1984 Nobel Lecture', text available in Allen (ed.), *Archbishop Desmond Tutu*, pp. 84–92, at p. 92.

25 Allen (ed.), *Archbishop Desmond Tutu*, p. 97.

26 Desmond Tutu, 'Punitive Sanctions: Press Statement, 1986', text available in Allen (ed.), *Archbishop Desmond Tutu*, pp. 102–8, at p. 108.

27 John Allen (ed.), *Archbishop Desmond Tutu*, p. 110.

28 Edited parts of Tutu's sermon available in Allen (ed.), *Archbishop Desmond Tutu*, pp. 110–24, citation at p. 114.

29 For an excellent overview of churches involved in socio-political issues during this period, see Tristan Anne Borer, *Challenging the State: Churches as Political Actors in South Africa 1980–1994* (Notre Dame, IN: University of Notre Dame Press), 1998.

30 See Allen (ed.), *Archbishop Desmond Tutu*, p. 139.

31 For a general view on the role of Christianity within a post-apartheid and democratic South African society, see John W. De Gruchy, *Christianity and Democracy: A Theology for a Just World Order* (Cambridge: Cambridge University Press), 1995.

32 See different essays in Robert I. Rotberg and Dennis Thompson (eds), *Truth v. Justice: The Morality of Truth Commissions* (Princeton, NJ: Princeton University Press), 2000.

33 The cutting-off dates were from 1960 to 1993, subsequently extended to May 1994 – see Deborah Posel and Graeme Simpson, 'Introduction: the Power of Truth – South Africa's Truth and Reconciliation Commission in context', in *Commissioning the Past: Understanding South Africa's Truth and Reconciliation Commission* (Johannesburg: Witwatersrand University Press), 2002, pp. 1–13, at p. 3.

34 See <http://www.doj.gov.za/trc/legal/act9534.htm>.

35 John W. De Gruchy, *Reconciliation: Restoring Justice* (Cape Town: David Philip), 2002; cf. John Dugard, 'Dealing with Crimes of a Past Regime: is amnesty still an option?', *Leiden Journal of International Law* 12 (2000/4), pp. 1001–15.

36 Piers Pigou, 'False Promises and Wasted Opportunities? Inside South Africa's Truth and Reconciliation Commission', in Posel and Simpson, *Commissioning the Past*, p. 47.

37 For the Chilean Truth and Reconciliation Commission's findings, see *Report of the Chilean National Commission on Truth and Reconciliation*, 2 volumes (Notre Dame, IN: University of Notre Dame Press, in cooperation with Center for Civil and Human Rights, Notre Dame Law School), 1993.

38 Desmond Tutu, *No Future Without Forgiveness* (New York: Doubleday), 1999, p. 279.

39 Graeme Simpson, 'Tell No Lies, Claim No Easy Victories: a brief evaluation of South Africa's Truth and Reconciliation Commission', in Posel and Simpson, *Commissioning the Past*, p. 247.

40 *Ubuntu* has also been used within the pastoral study of trans-cultural counselling in the context of Zambia – see Philip Baxter

OFM Cap, 'From Ubuzungu to Ubuntu: resources for pastoral counselling in a Bantu context', Unpublished PhD thesis (Dublin: Kimmage Mission Institute), 2006.

41 Richard A. Wilson, *The Politics of Truth and Reconciliation in South Africa: Legitimizing the Post-Apartheid State* (Cambridge: Cambridge University Press), 2001, p. 9.

42 Tutu, *No Future Without Forgiveness*, and Michael Battle, *Reconciliation: The Ubuntu Theology of Desmond Tutu* (Cleveland, OH: Pilgrim Press), 1997.

43 See Allen (ed.), *Archbishop Desmond Tutu*, p. 197.

6 Mother Teresa of Calcutta

1 Christopher Hitchens, *The Missionary Position: Mother Teresa in Theory and Practice* (London and New York: Verso), 1995, p. 98.

2 The date 10 September is considered so important by the Missionaries of Charity that it is called 'Inspiration Day'.

3 Malcolm Muggeridge, *Something Beautiful for God* (New York: Harper & Row), 1971, and *Confessions of a Twentieth-Century Pilgrim* (San Francisco: Harper & Row), 1988.

4 See the limited understanding of Mother Teresa suggested by Christopher Hitchens, 'An Interview with Christopher Hitchens on Mother Teresa', *Free Inquiry*, Fall 1996, pp. 54–5.

5 Ronald Reagan, 'Remarks on presenting the Presidential Medal of Freedom to Mother Teresa', 20 June 1985, <www.medaloffreedom. com/MotherTeresa.htm>.

6 *Time*, 12 April 1989, pp. 11, 13.

7 Desmond Doig, *Mother Teresa: Her People and Her Work* (New York: Harper & Row), 1976, p. 156.

7 The body and contemplation

1 See Sallie McFague, *Models of God: Theology for an Ecological Nuclear Age* (London: SCM Press), 1987.

2 For works by Merton, see Chapter 1. The Fourteenth Dalai Lama's life is also well researched – see the excellent summary provided by Alexander Norman, 'The Fourteenth Dalai Lama Tenzin Gyatso', in Martin Brauen (ed.), *The Dalai Lamas: A Visual History* (Chicago: Serindia Publications), 2005, pp. 163–79; Michael Harris Goodman, *The Last Dalai Lama: A Biography* (London: Sidgwick & Jackson), 1986, and the Fourteenth Dalai Lama's autobiography, *Freedom in Exile: The Autobiography of His*

Holiness the Dalai Lama of Tibet (London: Hodder & Stoughton), 1990.

3 Thomas Merton, *The Asian Journal of Thomas Merton* (New York: New Directions), 1975, p. 112.

4 The Fourteenth Dalai Lama, *Freedom in Exile*, p. 208.

5 John Dear, *Peace Behind Bars: A Peacemaking Priest's Journal from Jail* (Franklin, WI: Sheed & Ward), 1995, p. 65.

6 John Powers (ed.), *Wisdom of Buddha: The Samdhinirmocana Mahayana Sutra* (Berkeley, CA: Dharma Publishing), 1995, p. 385.

7 Dear, *Peace Behind Bars*, p. 65.

8 The Roman coin, the silver denarius (worth a daily wage – Matthew 20.2), had the image of the emperor on it, following a Roman practice of engraving human likeness, a practice that was rejected by the Jews (Exodus 20.3), who used small copper coins. If commentators are correct, and the coin was minted by Tiberius in the 20s, its legend read TI CAESAR DIVI AVG F AVGVSTUS ('Tiberius Caesar Augustus, Son of Divine Augustus'), thus proclaiming the divinity of the Roman Emperor – see Craig A. Evans, 'Mark 8.27—16.20', in *World Biblical Commentary*, Vol. 34 B (Nashville, TN: Thomas Nelson), 2001, p. 247.

9 See Mario I. Aguilar, 'The Archaeology of Memory and the Issue of Colonialism: Mimesis and the Controversial Tribute to Caesar in Mark 12.13–17', *Biblical Theology Bulletin* 35 (2), 2005, pp. 60–6.

10 The Romans had imposed forced taxation (χῆνσος) in 6 CE, when Judea, Samaria and Idumea were placed under Roman occupation. Judas and others revolted against such taxation (Acts 5.37), which implied the partition of Jewish land, a policy that led to the creation of the Zealot movement and the rising of 70 CE (Josephus, *Antiquities* XVIII:1.1, 6). It was therefore unlawful to suggest that taxes to Rome were not to be paid, and contentious within a Jewish milieu to suggest that taxes to the oppressors should be paid.

11 Carlos Bravo, 'Jesus of Nazareth, Christ the Liberator', in Ignacio Ellacuría and Jon Sobrino (eds), *Mysterium Liberationis: Fundamental Concepts of Liberation Theology* (Maryknoll, NY: Orbis), 1993, pp. 420–39, at p. 433. Bravo (1938–97), a Jesuit, born in Guadalajara, Mexico, was editor of the journal *Christus* and Professor of New Testament in the Jesuit Theological Institute in Mexico City.

12 Thomas Merton, *Contemplative Prayer* (London: Darton, Longman & Todd), 2005.

8 The Eucharist and politics

1 Daniel Berrigan took part in the filming of *The Mission*, and appears in the opening scenes with other Jesuits, opposite the falls. Berrigan decided to take part in order to experience the oppressive history of the Latin American indigenous peoples, and wrote a journal of his own feelings and impressions – see Daniel Berrigan, *The Mission: A Film Journal* (New York: Harper & Row), 1986.

2 I am aware that there are many reformed communities where the Eucharist is not celebrated at all and where the service of the Word informs worship, Christian life and social involvement. Thus, without ignoring that particular experience, I concentrate on those communities that have reached a social involvement and sometimes a political commitment based on their Eucharistic contemplation.

3 William T. Cavanaugh, *Torture and Eucharist: Theology, Politics and the Body of Christ* (Oxford: Blackwell), 1998, p. 12.

4 Cavanaugh, *Torture and Eucharist*, p. 11.

5 Mario I. Aguilar, *A Social History of the Catholic Church in Chile I: The First Period of the Military Government 1973–1980*; *II: The Pinochet Government and Cardinal Raúl Silva Henriquez 1907–1999*; *III: The Second Period of the Military Government 1980–1990* (Lewiston, NY, Queenston, Ontario and Lampeter, Wales: Edwin Mellen Press), 2004, 2006.

6 Rosemary Radford Ruether, 'The Holocaust: theological and ethical reflections', in Gregory Baum (ed.), *The Twentieth Century: A Theological Overview* (Maryknoll, NY: Orbis; London: Geoffrey Chapman; Ottawa: Novalis), 1999, pp. 76–90.

7 That is the only possible approach to contemporary challenges to human goodness such as the 1994 Rwanda genocide – see Mario I. Aguilar, *The Rwanda Genocide and the Call to Deepen Christianity in Africa* (Eldoret, Kenya: AMECEA Gaba Publications), 1998.

8 The importance of the body in theology has been emphasized recently by inculturation theologies in Africa and Latin America, where dances and body gestures have become incorporated into a theological discourse related to the salvific plan of God in a particular context – see François Kabasele-Lumbala, *Celebrating Jesus*

Christ in Africa (Maryknoll, NY: Orbis), 1997; Diego Irarrázaval, *Inculturation: New Dawn of the Church in Latin America* (Maryknoll, NY: Orbis), 2000; and *Rito y pensar cristiano* (Lima: Centro de Estudios y Publicaciones), 1993.

9 José Miguez Bonino, 'Love and Social Transformation in Liberation Theology', in March H. Ellis and Otto Maduro (eds), *The Future of Liberation Theology: Essays in Honor of Gustavo Gutiérrez* (Maryknoll, NY: Orbis), 1989, pp. 121–8, at p. 123. Bonino, Argentinian Methodist theologian and professor at the Instituto Superior Evangélico de Estudios Teológicos (ISEDET) in Buenos Aires, was born in Rosario de Santa Fe in 1924 – see Mario I. Aguilar, *The History and Politics of Latin American Theology*, vol. 1 (London: SCM Press), 2007, pp. 56–71.

10 Leonardo Boff, *Ecclesiogenesis: The Base Communities Reinvent the Church* (Maryknoll, NY: Orbis), 1986, p. 41. Boff, born in Concordia, Brazil, in 1938, is one of the best-known theologians of liberation, and currently teaches at the University of the State of Rio de Janeiro. He has published more than 60 books – see Aguilar, *History and Politics*, vol. 1, pp. 121–36.

11 Boff, *Ecclesiogenesis*.

12 Johannes H. Emminghaus, *The Eucharist: Essence, Form, Celebration* (Collegeville, MN: Liturgical Press), 1978, p. xxiii.

13 Nicholas Buxton, 'A Month of Sundays', *The Tablet*, 3 December 2005, pp. 20–1, at p. 20.

14 Mario I. Aguilar, *Cardenal Raúl Silva Henríquez: Presencia en la Vida de Chile 1907–1999* (Santiago: Editorial Copygraph), 2004, p. 210.

15 Reinaldo Sapag, oral communication, Santiago, Friday 11 November 2005.

16 Archbishop Juan Francisco Sarasti Jaramillo, CIM, Archbishop of Cali, Colombia, 'Bread of Life, Culture of Death', *L'Osservatore Romano* (weekly edn) 42, 19 October 2005, p. 15.

9 Lay contemplatives and voters

1 Abbot Christopher Jamison, *Finding Sanctuary: Monastic Steps for Everyday Life* (London: Weidenfeld & Nicolson), 2006, p. 44.

2 Thomas Merton, *Thomas Merton on St Bernard*, Cistercian Studies Series 9 (Kalamazoo, MI: Cistercian Publications; London and Oxford: A. R. Mowbray), 1980, p. 70.

3 Leonardo Boff, *Cry of the Earth, Cry of the Poor* (Maryknoll, NY: Orbis), 1997, p. 115.

4 Michael Mott, *The Seven Mountains of Thomas Merton* (London: Sheldon Press), 1984, p. 214.

5 Judith Hunter, 'Exploding the Argument: the Mim tea estate and Polonnaruwa', *The Merton Journal* 14 (2007/1), pp. 17–27, at p. 26.

6 Robert Inchausti, 'Beyond Political Illusion: the role of the individual in troubled times', in Angus Stuart (ed.), *The World in my Bloodstream*, Papers presented at the Fourth General Conference of the Thomas Merton Society of Great Britain and Ireland at Oakham School, April 2002 (Abergavenny, Monmouthshire: Three Peaks Press), 2004, pp. 27–39, at p. 27.

7 Leonardo Boff, *Fundamentalism, Terrorism and the Future of Humanity* (London: SPCK), 2006, p. 30.

Index